From Power Struggles to
Conflict Resolution

Dear Nicole —
The success of kids absolutely
begins with the commitment,
passion, and love of a school
leader. Congrats on making a
difference at a whole new level!
Feel free to reach out if I can
support you!

From Power Struggles to Conflict Resolution

Transform Your School's Culture Today

Janice Case

ROWMAN & LITTLEFIELD
Lanham • Boulder • New York • London

Published by Rowman & Littlefield
A wholly owned subsidiary of The Rowman & Littlefield Publishing Group, Inc.
4501 Forbes Boulevard, Suite 200, Lanham, Maryland 20706
www.rowman.com

Unit A, Whitacre Mews, 26-34 Stannary Street, London SE11 4AB

British Library Cataloguing in Publication Information Available

Library of Congress Cataloging-in-Publication Data

ISBN 978-1-4758-2196-3 (cloth : alk. paper) -- ISBN 978-1-4758-2197-0 (pbk. : alk. paper) -- ISBN
978-1-4758-2198-7 (electronic)

∞ ™ The paper used in this publication meets the minimum requirements of American
National Standard for Information Sciences Permanence of Paper for Printed Library
Materials, ANSI/NISO Z39.48-1992.

Printed in the United States of America

Contents

Acknowledgments

I could never have foreseen when I published an article on power struggles ("Winning the War Against Power Struggles: Adults as Learners and Role Models," which appeared in the February 2015 issue of *Principal Leadership*) that I would end up here, officially able to add the title "author" to my list of experiences. When I was approached to expand my ideas in that article, I was at first humbled that anyone would think I could make the leap and then excited to take on the challenge. My first thank you, then, has to go to the folks at Rowman & Littlefield for having the vision for this book and for rolling up their sleeves and tackling the work alongside of me.

The fact is, many a school leader thinks to themselves at one time or another "I gotta write a book." To be quite frank, that sentiment is often followed by a "You just can't make this stuff up." If you're a school leader (or any educator for that matter) reading this right now, you're nodding and thinking "amen!" What a complete and utter rush, then, to actually get to do it.

It has been a privilege to have the opportunity to put pen to paper (I mean fingers to keyboard) and share my experiences and strategies on this topic. Ultimately, I believe completely that the key to making schools better—whether your school is deemed struggling, or failing, or even successful—is improving culture. You cannot improve student achievement, and we all strive to improve student achievement, without taking a close look at the system of beliefs that drive a school as well as the outcomes that are a direct result of those beliefs. Likewise, you cannot take a deep dive into this or any topic without a specific, concrete plan of action.

This book was written to serve that purpose—to be a specific, concrete resource for a plan of action for school leaders to tackle the very targeted problem of power struggles and conflict chipping at, or even tearing away of, any sense of positive school culture. There is absolutely a place for theory and research, and much can be found in the area of creating a positive school culture. This book is different because it acknowledges that school leaders facing the very unique challenges of education today need answers. Even more, they need answers customized to fit their school, embedded in resources like this one with a roadmap for implementation.

I have never met a school principal who didn't want to be better. I have met plenty of school principals who wanted to be better and simply didn't know how. This book is designed to fill that gap in this focused area. I would be remiss, then, if I didn't also thank you, the readers for considering this book a worthwhile expense. I know you won't be sorry for taking the leap.

As I said, I could never have foreseen ending up here. Nor could I have guessed when I agreed to write this book that the hardest part would be the acknowledgments. Seriously, how do you succinctly and yet comprehensively thank anyone and everyone who helped you get here? For me to do that, here in the first of what I hope will be many publications, I would have to thank every person who ever had an influence on my becoming an educator, anyone who encouraged and supported me as I moved into school leadership, anyone who gave me opportunities along the way that led to my providing professional learning to other educators, and the friends who kept it real for me along the way. You can perhaps imagine how long that list would be and, yes, I would absolutely be guaranteed to forget someone.

So to make this simple, and to ensure an attempt at no hard feelings, please know that if you are reading this, and you fit any of these criteria, I am thinking of you in this moment, this very second of writing this acknowledgment, and I am grateful for you. I am grateful for the opportunities you provided, I am thankful for the guidance you showed, I am grateful for your unwavering friendship, and I am most grateful for the many ways in which you let me into your life because I learned so much from each and every one of you.

More formally, I would thank the National Association of Secondary School Principals (and its state affiliate Virginia Association of Secondary School Principals) for considering my article last winter and for deciding it was good enough to publish. That decision did, after all, result in my ideas getting noticed. Consequently, I have to thank Rosalind Wiseman and Charles Kuhn for being my editors of both the writing and content of that article—our many brainstorming sessions resulted in a piece that did exactly what I set out to do: help school leaders.

There is no doubt that kids, kids from all walks of life, kids who love school and kids who hate it, kids who hugged me every day in the hallways of my buildings and those who likely didn't love me for a whole myriad of reasons . . . ; each of these kids, every single one of them, had an influence on me as a leader, as a mom, as a person. Thank you to each of you for partnering with me to navigate the crazy world of teaching and learning. I love you guys.

On a personal level, words cannot describe my gratitude for my family and their support. I have several members of my extended family who have been critical to my success both as a school leader over the last fifteen years and as I made the transition to consultant. Your commitment to our core family allowed me to be gone, simply stated, because as a school leader you are often "gone" from your own family in order to support hundreds and even thousands of other children and other families. You don't do that without a cost to your own family. My cost was minimized because of the family members who stepped up to fill the void. . . . Thank you for that.

Over the years my daughters, Montana and Sydney, would often ask why I had to do this job, why couldn't someone else's mom or dad do it instead. This question often came when I had to miss something special to be at school or after the thousandth time of their being dragged to school with me for yet another event. My response was always the same: We all have a moral obligation to serve in some capacity at some point in our lives. This was my way to serve and, consequently, theirs because they too sacrificed to make it work. To them I can only say that being your mom has been my most important role in this life, and know that your sacrifices resulted in the lives of so many others being improved. Thank you for that.

Montana and Sydney have been joined now by their stepsiblings, Brandon, Layni, Jonah, and Camy. To say our new blended family is unconventional, well that would be an understatement. And yet that new blended family has taught me so much more about relationships; sometimes you just don't know what you don't know. I thank our four new additions for jumping in and joining with us to work to make our family work. That means more to me than you'll ever know.

My husband, Joe . . . I don't think he knew what he was getting into when he married this principal turned consultant. One of the many things I love about him, though, is that he was all in from the beginning and is the first to say, "You should do it" to whatever new opportunity I find or want to explore. That right there is just invaluable. Thank you for that. I love you more than words can say.

Finally, as educators, we can all look back and identify that one person, the one who is undoubtedly the reason we are where we are today. I was put on this path by a woman who understood who I was as a person (probably long before I understood myself) and, as a result of her own experience as an educator, sat me down one day and said, "You need to be a school principal." This was before I ever set foot in a classroom. She modeled courage, and strength, and a sheer will to overcome all obstacles to do what's best for kids. It is because of her that I knew from the beginning that the right answer always ended with "because it's what's best for kids." It's amazing how simple being an educator becomes when you bring it all back to that one simple statement. For that I will always be grateful to you, Joan L. Curcio. Know that your legacy lives on in me and so many others.

Foreword

Four years ago I walked through the halls of Potomac Falls High School looking for the principal. As I dodged students and tried to flow with the controlled chaos around me, I thought how simultaneously challenging and awesome it must be to lead this school. Potomac Falls High School, located in northern Virginia, had 1,500 students from all different backgrounds. From children living in huge suburban mansions to homeless shelters, first-generation immigrants studying side by side with students whose families had been in Virginia for generations, the student body was truly diverse. Moreover, like many schools, in addition to academics there was theater, band, athletics, and all kinds of clubs. The list of things going on in this school was endless. Behind every one of these programs faculty and students had to work together.

At the intersection of two hallways, calmly doing ten things at once, I saw the only person who could be the principal, Janice Case. Somehow she was able to connect with individual students as they walked by while talking into her walkie-talkie with the school's SRO. I remember shouting through the crowd of students, "It's really nice to meet you but I can come back later." "No, no it's fine," she responded. "Just give me two minutes."

She was right. Two minutes later the passing period was over and the halls were clear. When Janice introduced herself I immediately I knew this was a principal I wanted to work with. At first meeting anyone could tell she was fair, wanted the best of her students, had a great sense of humor, and…you didn't want to mess with her. I actually remember in those first moments imagining what it would be like to be a student sitting in her office trying to deceive her. Just the thought made me queasy.

The book you are about to read is born from the wisdom this administrator has gained in her years of daily experience working in schools. It also challenges and exposes the critical power dynamics that often undermine a school's culture. It's honest about how adults can contribute to a school culture where students are disengaged. It recognizes that there are some adults who believe the best way to educate children is to get them to comply to whatever they say and any resistance justifies escalation and punishment.

But it also recognizes the common yet really difficult obstacles educators face. Because the fact is you may love working with young people but it can be really hard to work with them. Some are amazingly good at knowing what buttons to push and how to undermine an adult's credibility. They fight you when you have no interest in battling. They resist when you just really need them to cooperate. Understandably, any educator will have moments where it's hard to respond effectively. As an administrator, how do you hold an adult accountable who is disrespectful to students? How do you teach adults how to be ethical authority figures so the students in their charge truly feel that they are part of a community, they are valued as individuals, and still must be held accountable to community rules? How do you work in partnership with your school resource officers? How do you engage young people in understanding their rights and responsibilities to others in the school community? Janice has given you the tools here to answer all these questions.

How an administrator works with the adults in the school will make or break a school culture. Any school can create and maintain a culture of dignity if the adults fundamentally believe that their authority and credibility is based on mutual respect between adults and young people. And there's no expectation of being perfect. It's the process that makes people believe in a leadership's competence and values. The process is hard but it's worth doing. You can't build a school community where children can truly engage in the learning process and teachers feel respected without it.

—**Rosalind Wiseman**, Educator and *New York Times* Bestselling Author
of *Queen Bees and Wannabes: Helping Your Daughter Survive Cliques,
Gossip, Boyfriends, and the New Realities of Girl World* and *Masterminds
and Wingmen: Helping Our Boys Cope with Schoolyard Power, Locker-
Room Tests, Girlfriends, and the New Rules of Boy World*

Chapter One

Power Struggles and School Culture: Start with Why

Congratulations! As a school leader, you have identified a challenge that exists within your school and have chosen to use this book as a resource to tackle it. That is, after all, what we do, right? We identify problems and strategically set about identifying and implementing solutions to those problems. Having been a school leader in K–12 environments, both private and public, your author knows too well our role as problem solvers. It is the compilation of that experience, as well as that of thousands of school leaders, upon which this book is based.

Let's acknowledge right up front, however, that this resource is not intended only for school principals. Anyone who plays a role in a school where power struggles are eating away at school culture will find this resource helpful. Though we target the school leader in the instruction, other staff will benefit from a direct reading of the text as well as through implementing the strategies included.

Sometimes when you see a problem and are not in the "official" role to address it, you can begin to feel helpless and frustrated. This resource is designed to support even the smallest effort to make a difference. There is no question that one small step by one person in a school can create a large-scale impact on a school's culture.

THE LEARNING

In this book we're going to spend time learning and sharing about school culture and how power struggles can work to erode any positives you've built, unless you tackle them head on. We will not spend time reviewing the research on school culture. We will not espouse on the obvious—school culture matters. You know this already or you wouldn't have selected this resource. There's no need to convince you that your school culture is having a direct impact on your students' achievement, for better or for worse. You know that already. All of that said, by all means, seek out a definition for school culture if you'd like.

In fact, simply google the term "school culture" and you'll quickly get a plethora of resources that will happily go on for pages and pages defining school culture. The common denominator is the idea that school culture encompasses all of the beliefs, traditions, norms, and so on that impact the day-to-day workings of a school. Seems simple, right? But we all know that in reality it's not so simple. You see, the common denominator to all of the components of school culture is *people*. And the fact is, when we are talking about people, there is just nothing simple about it.

Countless outstanding resources exist that address the importance of school culture especially as it pertains to student achievement and school success. The universal consensus is that a positive school culture equals increased student achievement and that, likewise, a negative school culture equals decreased student achievement. Certainly it's simple to garner the "appropriate" response from school leaders when faced with the question "How important is school culture?"

Most school leaders will answer emphatically that school culture is the most important component to a school's success. As leaders, we will go on to say that school culture is pervasive—you can feel it when you walk through the front doors. We'll elaborate with great detail about all of the things we can change to make a more positive school culture. In other words, we'll immerse ourselves in the "what" and the "how" of school culture. It's what we do.

THE WHATS

The fact is, when asked about school culture, we go right to the new paint job, the bright posters with positive messages, even the school-wide behavior models we've implemented. All of these "whats" are well and good and important to your school environment. Of greater importance, however, is going beyond the "whats" to really understand the "whys" of school culture. Why did we choose any of these options? Why specifically is the implementation of this particular school-wide behavior plan going to make a difference? Understanding why we succeed or don't succeed on any front is critical to our ability to actually make real change, the kind of real change that can translate to greater gains by our teachers and students.

The first step: understanding why our school culture is what it is. Have you taken the time, before launching all of your new initiatives, to simply understand how your culture is perceived and the reasons behind that perception? If not, that's your starting point. So how do you do that? The simplest method seems to be the use of surveys. Yes, collect the data.

Many of you likely have conducted such surveys. You've asked a strategic set of questions of your various stakeholder groups to better understand their perceptions of the school as a whole. You've provided the opportunity for stakeholders (teachers, students, parents, community members, etc.) to provide their feedback anonymously, and you gather the data regularly, at least two times per year, to monitor closely the impact of your leadership on your school's culture. If you haven't taken this step, now is the time.

The result—now you have the "what." Now you know *what* your stakeholders really think about the school's culture. Know that your school culture is likely to be perceived differently by different stakeholder groups. You'll have your share of disgruntled respondents—you know, the ones who claim you don't do anything right. Likewise, you'll have your share of "everything is perfect" respondents. In their eyes, you can't do anything wrong.

The key, of course, is to sort through all of those and seek a clear understanding of the truly insightful respondents—those folks who are paying close attention, who see the strengths *and* the weaknesses, and who can share their perceptions frankly and without judgment. This is the data that will be most useful as you take the next big step—understanding the "why."

THE WHYS

The whys are tough. The whys are where you and your team set your collective egos aside and acknowledge there are areas in which to grow. This is the point at which you rip off the Band-Aid and seek to understand why your stakeholders feel the way they do about any particular part of your school culture. The good news is that there are a lot of avenues to better understanding. Frankly, you and your school team are the best resource for making sense of the whys. You are out there every day observing the goings on of your school.

The adults in the building are responsible for how routines and processes are established and implemented. The adults in the building control inner workings, as it were. If you haven't already, it's time to embrace the idea that the adults in the building are the single most deciding factor, the answer to the question "why" of your school culture. At the end of the day, it is the interaction that adults have with one another as well as with students that makes or breaks a school culture.

Many of you are thinking right now that it's the kids who influence the school culture the most. "Our kids _____." Fill in the blank with your reason for why it's the *kids* who make the school culture negative: our kids are from low socioeconomic backgrounds; our kids are from single-parent homes; our kids are live in drug-infested neighborhoods; our kids are from high socioeconomic backgrounds and, therefore, are entitled; our kids have cultural differences that result in increased confrontation; our kids don't care about school and so don't get involved; our kids are only here seven hours a day and so its their parents' fault. . . . We could go on and on.

Interestingly enough, all of those excuses or "whys" are things school staff cannot control. These whys become really convenient when a school wrongly embraces the notion that if we can't control it, then we can't be held responsible for it, right? Wrong. Much like the changing trends in student achievement that show that students can succeed despite these mitigating factors, it is true that a school's culture can be overwhelmingly positive despite these mitigating factors. So what's the difference? Just like in schools where students achieve academically despite these obstacles, the difference is the people. The difference is the adults.

We are at a critical crossroads where the adults in schools must accept responsibility for the fact that they drive the school's culture in order to create positive change. But don't worry—there's a huge advantage as well. If the adults drive the culture, then it stands to reason that the adults have the ability to change the school culture. It can be done.

WHY THIS BOOK AND WHY NOW?

We know that school culture is a large spectrum composed of many facets of a school. This book cannot possibly address every "why" you discover as you peel back the layers of your school culture and better understand where it can be changed for the better. In fact, many resources designed to support school improvement fail (if failure is defined as not having the desired effect) because they are so broad. With broadness comes the tendency to offer general, wide-sweeping recommendations for improvement. In this resource, we could have, for example, attempted to identify as many "whys" as possible and pinpoint for you the reason any particular "why" is a problem and encourage you to fix that "why."

As a school leader who has experienced a fair share of ineffective professional learning experiences, the conclusion is that what school leaders need most is specific, guided direction on how to address an identified obstacle. It does you no good to hear the ideas on the "why" included in this resource if you do not leave this reading armed with an actual tool to use to *improve* the "why." The most effective tool you can receive is something that you can turn right around and implement with your school team immediately. As a result, this resource focuses on one *specific* why—the existence of power struggles.

For the sake of this resource, we will define power struggle as an interaction between two or more people where one person is trying to control another in order to be the dominant person in the interaction and to get the subordinate to comply. Power struggles were chosen as the one "why" to address in this book based on years of experience as a school leader as well as experiences with thousands of school leaders across the country. There is no doubt that power struggles and the conflict they create are pervasive in schools and, unless addressed, chip away at all facets of your school culture. School culture cannot be positive when power struggles are permitted to exist.

The interactions, both brief and extended, that occur between adults and children throughout the course of a day, a month, or a school year matter because they are the single most impactful way in which adults effectively communicate and demonstrate a positive culture to the students. It is in these fleeting moments that school culture is reinforced and the authority of adults is either respected and affirmed or resented. In these situations, the adult will either convey a culture based on power and control or a culture built on personal responsibility and dignity. In schools, our conversations about bullying and social justice, for example, often focus on student behavior, but the focus should also be on how adults treat each other and the students.

IT STARTS WITH YOU

The most effective leaders first reflect on how they react to these challenges and how to improve their responses, and then guide other adults on how to transform potential power struggles between students and adults, as well as between two adults, into positive interactions. One common way student and adult dignity is compromised in the school setting is through power struggles. So, what can we do about it?

Essential to your success is your ability to coach your team and your students about power struggles. To that end, this book is about helping you both to honestly assess your own ability in this area and to build your capacity to lead your school team in the effort to eliminate power struggles. The hope is that you chose this book because you, too, see power struggles as an obstacle in schools and are seeking to learn how to eliminate them. If so, you've come to the right place.

Chapters 1 and 2 set the stage for our work. Chapters 3 through 6 target the variety of ways that power struggles are carried out in schools. These chapters all follow a similar learning structure: vignette(s), alternative approaches or solutions to consider on coaching staff through these power struggles, and a discussion on how this particular type of power struggle impacts student learning. All of the solutions correlate to the lesson plan for professional development offered in chapter 8.

Note also that the variety of vignettes is strategic in that they are based on real-life scenarios, include K–12 environments, and offer an array of scenarios from which the leader can choose when planning the professional development for staff. Now let's take a closer look at the breakdown of each chapter.

Chapter 1: Power Struggles and School Culture: Start with Why. The nature of the relationships among the people who make up schools is at the heart of a positive or negative school culture. For this reason, then, it stands to reason that how people interact with one another has a direct impact on school culture and student achievement. Chapter 1 introduces the concept of the power struggle, acknowledges a common definition of school culture and a power struggle, and establishes a framework for our work together via this book.

Chapter 2: The Role of the School Leader in Eliminating Power Struggles. Now that both school culture and power struggles have been defined, it is time to make a deliberate connection to the school leader. Chapter 2 shows the reader how power struggles, left unaddressed, can chip away at the overall culture of a school and provides the reader with an understanding of the correlation of school leadership to school culture.

The author then walks the reader through how the influence of the school leader can positively or negatively affect school culture. This walk includes supporting the school leader in identifying when he or she becomes caught up in power struggles and how this negatively impacts the culture of the school. Finally, the reader gains a clear understanding of the responsibility that lies with the school leader in acknowledging that power struggles occur, modeling how to avoid power struggles, and teaching others to do the same.

Chapter 3: The Classroom as Battleground: Teacher vs. Student. In chapter 3, we begin our series of vignettes. We will focus in this chapter on classroom management and how teachers can both protect instructional time and preserve their relationship with students by avoiding power struggles in their day-to-day interactions with students.

Chapter 4: From Start to Finish: Power Struggles That Impact Student Learning throughout the Day. Chapter 4 provides an overview of how school culture is forged through every interaction a student has throughout his or her day. From the moment a student steps on the bus and is greeted by the bus driver to his or her encounter with the cafeteria staff, from the conversation with the school resource officer to the passing comment of a hall monitor, there are innumerable adults and, therefore interactions, ahead of the student each day.

To that end, it is important that the school leader include all staff in learning about the conflict that arises with power struggles. This means tailoring the professional development to meet the needs of all staff and, more than ever, being sure to walk the walk.

Chapter 5: Parents and School Staff: Power Struggles That Foster the Us vs. Them Culture. Parents are other stakeholders who highly influence school culture. Whether the helicopter parent or the parent who never crosses the threshold of the school, make no mistake—parents have a direct influence on your school culture. Chapter 5, which is structured like chapters 3, 4, and 6, draws connections for the reader to how parents influence school culture, on campus and off campus. In this chapter, the author offers strategies to use to draw parents in and make them champions of the school, thereby eliminating the "Us vs. Them" culture and replacing it with a "We" culture.

Chapter 6: Staff Cliques: When Power Struggles Threaten Staff Unity. It is important to acknowledge the impact that the relationships between staff has on school culture. Chapter 6 discusses openly the negative relationships that can exist between staff (some examples include veteran to new staff, inclusion or co-teacher relationships, teacher cliques in a grade level or department, etc.). Further, it supports the school leader in both how to acknowledge these relationships and how to lead staff to solutions designed to resolve the conflicts that are often at the root of these relationships.

Chapter 7: Leading the Learning with Your Students: Coaching Your Students to Avoid Power Struggles. Providing professional development to staff on power struggles is addressing only one piece of the puzzle. The other critical piece is the student. Chapter 7 focuses on the role of the student both in power struggles that involve adults as well as those that involve other students. The chapter offers ways in which the school leader can address students about power struggles to include partnering with the student leadership council to create new ways to teach students that are most likely to get their attention.

Chapter 8: Leading the Learning: Your Professional Development Guide. Chapter 8 brings us all of the way back to the beginning and our emphasis on the critical role that a positive school culture plays in school transformation and school success. Now that the reader is armed with multiple vignettes to reference to use with both adults and students, chapter 8 brings all of the pieces together into a specific lesson plan, designed to be implemented by the school leader with a variety of stakeholder groups, in order to start the dialogue about power struggles and, thereby, begin the work of eliminating them at the classroom and school level.

WRAP-UP

Before we jump in, let's also establish a common understanding of some key terms. Oftentimes in schools these terms are used interchangeably or even mean something different from school to school. To avoid confusion, note the following designations:

- **Administrative Team (or Admin Team):** team in the school composed of the principal and any other designated administrators like assistant principals, deans, and so on.
- **Leadership Team:** team in the school composed of the admin team plus other key stakeholder representatives like department heads, grade-level leads, parent representatives, student representatives, and so on.
- **School Team:** all of the adults who make up your school staff.

Now that we've broken down the journey upon which you are about to embark, you'll have a better idea of where we will start, where we are going, and how we will get there. There you have it from start to finish. Shall we begin?

Chapter Two

The Role of the School Leader in Eliminating Power Struggles

Derek is in the hallway during class time and is wearing his hat (a violation of the school dress code policy). Mr. Smith sees Derek in the hall. Although he's never had Derek in class, he has frequently addressed Derek's insistence on wearing a hat. As Derek passes by two other adults, Mr. Smith calls out to him, demanding that he take the hat off immediately. Derek ignores him and keeps walking.

Mr. Smith calls out again, this time louder, and includes a threat ("If you don't take off that hat, you'll go to the office."). Derek stops and proceeds to challenge Mr. Smith about how "You're the only person who ever says anything" and "My teacher lets me wear my hat," and so on. Mr. Smith now moves in front of Derek. Their verbal exchange becomes increasingly heated and culminates in Mr. Smith demanding that Derek go to the office. Mr. Smith then writes Derek up for defiance.

This is a typical scenario that occurs in schools every day. If you were Mr. Smith's supervisor, you could perceive it as a simple disciplinary referral for violating the dress code, or you could see it as a power struggle that negatively contributes to your school culture. Power struggles occur between adults and students, as well as adults and other adults, and they can occur across all stakeholder groups. It's important that all groups see your commitment to eliminating power struggles by your efforts to help everyone learn better options.

IT STARTS WITH YOU

Inherent in addressing this problem is your ability as the school leader to assess your own influence when it comes to power struggles. Who better to use power struggles in their day-to-day interactions than the school leader him- or herself? After all, you have the title to support a "do it my way" mentality, right? Here, right here in this moment, is the time for a gut check. How do you interact with your various stakeholder groups? Take your school team, for example; do you tend to shut them down, excusing your behavior with the thought that this is simply to accomplish the work more efficiently? After all, at some point you just have to make the decision, right?

So what about kids? Do you have a "because I said so" mentality, or do you approach student discipline, for example, as an opportunity to understand a student's behavior rather than to control it? When you are observed interacting with students, do you appear to be protecting the students' dignity or using tactics that are humiliating in nature?

Even tougher, how do you proceed with scenarios that involve a staff member and a student, both of whom are looking to you for resolution? Can both the staff member and the student count on you to collaborate to find compromise, or does the student know going in that you will pick sides and have the staff member's back despite whether or not it is warranted?

Answers to these questions are critical. You cannot lead the learning of eliminating power struggles if you, in fact, engage in power struggles yourself. Understanding how you are perceived is the first step. If you answered *yes* to any of the questions above, then you have a problem, one that must be solved before you can proceed. But it's okay! We cannot be perfect in all things all of the time. Being willing to engage in self-improvement is a powerful characteristic of some of the most effective leaders in schools today.

Be mindful that your self-reflection is important. The fact that your staff sees you engaged in self-reflection can be powerful. Just as important, however, is how others perceive you. Though you may answer the three questions one way, would your staff and the students you serve agree with your answers? The only way to know this is by being courageous enough to ask the questions of others. You have many ways to do this, but we'll look at a couple of specific options here.

Soliciting Opinions from Students

Let's start with students. Your relationships with various student groups will be critical here. If you have close ties to your student government group, then you can engage in this reflection with them to get feedback from the student view. Depending on the nature of your relationship with this group, you can do this via discussion or via a written-response survey.

You are looking for something simple that gets to the heart of your question—how do students perceive you? Specifically, how do they perceive your beliefs about the relationships between students and adults in the school? For younger students or in environments where there are no student leadership groups, you might consider gathering this information with the help of a guidance counselor or teachers. These folks can conduct the verbal or written survey of students and then report the results back to you.

Soliciting Feedback from Adults

Understanding how adults perceive you is the next step. Your goal is to survey both the staff serving with you in your school as well as a trusted mentor who can provide you feedback from an administrator-to-administrator perspective. Surveys can be tricky. Essentially, you want to provide the opportunity for your team to provide feedback in a way that is nonthreatening (so that they will provide honest feedback) and that takes minimal time. If you do not already conduct a survey of your performance at least annually, now is the time to start. It's a simple concept, right?

Some of the most effective teachers are those who consistently survey their students for feedback on their teaching—not on the content, not on the materials, but specifically on their teaching methods and their ability to convey standards in a way that ensures that learning takes place. As a result, encouraging all teachers to conduct surveys of their students is a must but something you cannot do as the school leader unless you are modeling the same practice. Your rationale is the same; you are looking for your school team's feedback on your practice in order to know how to improve.

Getting the most out of your feedback tool means using carefully designed questions geared toward all of your targeted areas. For our purposes, you are asking questions designed to get an understanding of how staff members perceive your practices that involve interpersonal interactions like those that may or may not result in power struggles. It's always a good idea to ask two open-ended questions: one for recommendations and one for commendations. Be sure to provide the time for the survey in the context of an already scheduled staff meeting. In other words, don't ask folks to take their own time to do this—instead, give them some of your allocated time. Again, these small details model your value of each individual.

Using the Data

Now that you have feedback, what will you do with it? First, of course, you will absorb the feedback and begin to make some sense of how you are perceived. You'll have data-based evidence of the "what" of how you are perceived and will work to understand the "why" of these perceptions. For better or for worse, why do folks perceive you as they do? These answers will be your basis for beginning your work on power struggles.

Let's pause to discuss one more step you can take to maximize the impact of your survey data. It's important, whenever you survey a group for any purpose, to share the data with that group. In this case, be sure to carve out time with your team to review your data. In addition to sharing numbers, we suggest taking an additional telling step. Remember all of those recommendations you were given? That open-ended question was a place for individual staff members to share specific ways in which they believe you can improve as their leader. We have found that it's powerful to recruit your staff to give you guidance on how to turn their recommendations into action.

At that same meeting where you share your raw survey data, put the staff in groups and provide each group with a small number of your recommendations (remember, don't change the wording, don't modify them in any way, show folks what their colleagues said to you in its purest form; the exception, of course, is to leave out any identifying information or any comments that may have included sensitive information that would be inappropriate to share). Cut the recommendations into strips and give each group four or five to consider. Ask that as a group they discuss each recommendation and, on a provided index card, give you suggestions on how to improve in the identified area.

This activity serves two purposes. First, you'll get some outstanding ideas that will most likely far surpass any that you could have come up with on your own, again, harnessing the brain power of the group. Second, you'll witness the epiphanies as colleagues remark about what others said about your leadership—both their astonishment that you are perceived in certain ways as well as, in some cases, their consternation that others would say such things.

It's an epiphany among them that each of them perceives your leadership differently based on their own past experiences, their own biases. This epiphany is a powerful first step for any disgruntled staff to think about why they feel the way they do and how much of it truly is about you as the leader versus them as the team member.

Now that you have a sense from the staff, don't forget the other adult perception—that of a trusted mentor or colleague. This is a simple courageous conversation wherein you ask the questions posed early on here about how you interact with adults and students. This person should be someone who has walked in the shoes of school leader in the past and who has had the opportunity to observe you in action. It goes without saying that this person should be someone who will be brutally honest with you. You'll want to review the data gathered from your staff and students with this colleague and together work on ensuring that your understanding of the "why" is absolutely accurate.

After all of this, should you determine that you have some growing to do in the area of power struggles, you can use this book as your first step in a more productive direction. If you can embrace both the belief articulated here about the impact of power struggles on your school's culture and the approaches outlined to avoid power struggles, then you can begin to practice the strategies immediately.

Of utmost importance will be your candid acknowledgment of your own mistakes to both staff and students as you introduce the concept of eliminating power struggles. Your candor will go a long way toward earning the respect of stakeholders and garnering their approval of heading down this road as you work together to improve your school's culture. Once you have assessed your own skills in this aspect of school culture and have begun to strengthen your skill as necessary, it's time to shift your focus to your staff.

The Entire Team's Starting Point

First and foremost, it is critical to remind your school team that it takes two people for a power struggle to occur. The student cannot have a power struggle on his or her own. When people engage in a power struggle it is because they want to prove they have authority or that another person doesn't have power over them. Both participants want the other person to back down, and a battle ensues and continues until someone says or thinks, "I won. He backed off." Power struggles often have less to do with the *content* of the conflict than the *dynamics* between the people.

In addition, both participants quickly become aware of any audience— other students and faculty members who witness the situation. Once the power struggle begins, and an audience is present, the problem expands to "saving face" in front of others. Both participants may try to pull others into the conflict in an effort to intimidate the other person to acquiesce, which further heightens the likelihood that the situation will quickly escalate.

It's likely that you have team members who believe that their title alone and/or the fact that they are adults should be enough to demand young people's immediate acknowledgment and agreement to follow any direction or command. It is usually the case that adults with this mindset are the most volatile and are more likely to contribute to a negative school culture. Their need to "teach" the student to respect adults in the moment overpowers any sense of self-control. In this scenario, the adult will likely use a loud voice and an intimidating posture and will generally escalate the situation.

If the adult finds himself engaging in a power struggle for the purpose of exhibiting control, then no one wins. If the adult finds herself engaging in a power struggle because she is frustrated with repeatedly addressing the same issue over and over again, then no one wins. If the adult finds himself engaging in a power struggle because he is the adult and kids should listen, then no one wins.

It's especially important to clearly articulate how the adult loses in these situations. The adult loses when there are colleagues present who see the interaction and now are less likely to approach the adult because of his perceived unwillingness to work through conflict. The adult loses when student observers, perhaps kids who have a positive rapport in class with the adult, now see her in a different light—as someone willing to strip a student of his or her dignity. This new realization will follow into the classroom.

Not all adults will agree that this is a problem or area of concern because they believe that students should comply, no matter the circumstance. Some of your team members may be notorious for engaging in power struggles with other faculty or students and won't see themselves as a part of the problem. There are two ways to approach these folks. First, it helps to engage these individuals by using the notion "Have you or someone you know been in this situation with a student?" or "Even if you feel you rarely or never get into power struggles with students, it's likely you've witnessed someone else doing this, right?" By wording it this way, adults are less likely to get defensive.

Also, when you use an example of your own (this is where the modeling we mentioned before becomes important) or one from the vignettes provided to you in chapters 3 through 7, you are demonstrating that there is no shame in recognizing this behavior in yourself.

Second, convey the idea that we don't want kids to learn to comply with people just because they have more power based on age, title, position in the school, and so on. If we teach this, we send kids mixed messages. On the one hand, we are trying to teach kids to think for themselves (i.e., "don't cave to peer pressure") and then on the other we say things like, "Do what I say and don't question me."

If we want critically thinking brains, we have to allow kids to push back—respectfully. The kid who complies with an adult due to sheer dominance is the same kid using the same behavior pattern to comply with a peer who is doing something unethical. This is an opportunity to teach kids how to stand up for their beliefs in a respectful way.

WRAP-UP

It's important to acknowledge that you know power struggles exist in your school. It's equally important to reinforce that you know all of your team members want to improve and certainly never knowingly engage in a power struggle to be hurtful. Starting with you is the only way to begin. The impact you have through modeling self-reflection and modeling how to seek and implement improved practices is perhaps the most far-reaching action you can have in your role. Ultimately, your goal is to make it clear that you know what happens in your school, while also maintaining everyone's dignity—something else that you must always strive to model as the school leader.

Chapter Three

The Classroom as Battleground

Teacher vs. Student

Just as the title to this chapter suggests, power struggles in the classroom can create a veritable battleground with a teacher on one side and students on the other. It's no surprise that in this context there is likely very little learning happening. Students cannot learn in an environment riddled by a hierarchy designed to "keep students in their place" and make it clear that the teacher is dominant.

The simple fact is that students and support staff are your best resource for understanding if and with whom these classroom battles exist in your school. If you are maintaining a high level of visibility and presence in the classroom, then you already know this from direct observation. That said, your students and support staff could help you understand when these types of classroom battles are playing out in a manner that is subtle enough that you may be unaware of them.

Classroom management is a thoroughly explored topic in the arena of education research. There are no limits to the resources available for school leaders and teachers on how to most effectively manage a learning environment. Preferred techniques differ from school to school, and teacher to teacher. As the school leader you have a responsibility to be well versed in an array of classroom management approaches so that you can support staff at all levels.

For our purposes, we will focus on what we know is at the heart of classroom management—relationships. There is no shortage of evidence that supports the importance of positive relationships at both the classroom and whole-school level. We've learned over and over again the power of a student who feels connected to at least one adult in his school.

For the sake of our discussion, we define "feel connected" as when a student can identify at least one adult with whom he looks forward to sharing personal accomplishments, experiences, and failures. Who is the person at school, if there is someone, with whom the student can't wait to talk when he has news to share? This is the person, then, to whom he feels connected.

IT STARTS WITH YOU: THE LEARNING

Let's pause here and address the question of how you know whether your kids feel connected. We frequently have workshop participants ask for ideas on how to gauge the connectedness of their kids. We'll share two strategies that, when used together, paint a powerful picture of where your school stands by this measure. The first strategy involves gathering information from your students.

In your next survey of students regarding school culture, add the question, "Please write the name of 1 or 2 adults to whom you feel connected at school. This can be any adult despite his/her role. Note that by 'feel connected,' we mean an adult with whom you are excited to share news like personal accomplishments, an experience you had, or even something you're concerned about."

Generally, you conduct surveys anonymously. In order for this survey to give you as much information as necessary upon which to act, it's important that students actually put their names on it. To that end, you may want to have this as a separate activity from your regularly scheduled school culture survey in order to make students feel more comfortable with putting a name on it. Ultimately, you can decide to conduct it anonymously, but know that you will miss out on some of the strategies discussed here as a result.

While you are gathering this information, find a large bulletin board–sized space (preferably in a room with a door, like a conference room, so that it can be accessed by staff but is not out for public use) and have the names of every staff member (from custodians to cafeteria support, teachers to administrators, school psychologists, etc.—any staff member who has a regular presence in your school) listed with enough space next to each name to keep a tally. Leave space to add names at the end as you'll invariably forget to list someone that a student will identify.

Now that you're prepped and you've collected the student surveys, the next step is the most time-consuming and tedious, but it's important that you or a member of your administrative team do it. One by one, you'll take each survey document and, as a staff member's name is listed by a student, put a tally mark next to his or her name on the board you've created. Yes, you are creating a list that shows how many students self-report as feeling connected to a particular staff member.

As you go through the surveys, you are also identifying any students who could not name a staff member with whom they feel connected. If your students put their names on their surveys then you can turn these surveys over to counselors to follow up. Your team is going to want to better understand why certain students don't feel connected to anyone.

Your finished product at this stage is a board that looks something like this:

Staff Name	Tally	Staff Name	Tally	Staff Name	Tally
Brown	₩₩	Jones	‖	Johnson	₩₩ ‖‖
Segway	₩₩ ₩₩	Roberts	‖	Juarez	‖‖
Whittaker	0	Danielson	₩₩ ₩₩ ‖‖‖	Barrod	0

Figure 3.1.

You're likely to find that as this work proceeds, your staff will start to notice that something is going on in the conference room. Word will get around and they'll begin asking what this is and what it's about. You'll have to decide how to share the purpose of the board. You can share as they ask, or you can wait until you're done and then communicate the purpose of the board to the entire staff.

The key is to reinforce the message to staff that the board is about understanding how kids perceive us. You will find that many of your staff will take this exercise to heart. They're going to have very different responses. Some will beat themselves up if the number of kids who identified them is smaller than they would have expected. This group perhaps feels they are more connected to students then they actually are—this is a great point of self-reflection for them. Still others will be pleasantly surprised; these are your staff members who are unaware of the positive impact they have on students. They're simply going about their day being the positive person they are, and they'll be pleased to see that it results in students feeling connected to them.

Another distinct group will be the staff members who get no tally marks; no students identify them as someone to whom they feel connected. You will likely not be surprised by who is in this group. For some of them, there will be surprise. For some of them, there will be indifference. For some of them, there will be guilt or humiliation.

Again, this cannot be stressed enough, it is *imperative* that you have contact with any staff member who has a negative reaction to the board regardless of his or her tallies. Your goal is never to humiliate but, instead, to lead the learning, lead the reflection process. Consider addressing the board by commenting on your own tallies. Did you receive any as the school leader? Some leaders will and some will not. How do your tallies make you feel? What reflections have they garnered in you? Share this with your staff, and it will go a long way toward supporting their own reflective process.

Now that you've taken care of your staff, open the discussion about what the students' responses to the prompt mean in general for your school. Remember, we started this part of our conversation with the general topic of classroom management. This strategy is designed to help you and your team better understand how you're doing on the front of relationships in your school. Big picture—if a large number of your students cannot identify an adult with whom they feel connected, then you have a challenge to address. If, however, the majority can identify an adult, this bodes well for your overall standing as a school team with respect to relationships.

Moving on to strategy two—we promised you two strategies to gauge relationships. This strategy targets your staff's perception and can take two formats. You could replicate the board you created for your student data but, instead, replace staff names with student names. Yes, list them all on one board. Next you would have staff (again, all staff, no matter their roles) visit the board and put a tally mark next to any student with whom they feel connected (using the same definition as above, this student comes to them to share, get support, etc.). You'll need a mechanism for checking staff members off as they complete the task to ensure that all are included.

An alternative format that allows you to accomplish two relationship-building activities at once is to create a stack of postcards, one for each student in the school. Leave the postcards blank except for the students' home addresses. At your next staff meeting, have the cards laid out alphabetically on tables so that they can be quickly perused. Let staff know that you want to surprise students with a positive note at a random time in the year. The note is not for any specific accomplishment but, instead, is just about sending the student an encouraging message. You intend for every student to get a postcard.

Ask staff to pick the postcards of students whom they feel would identify them as being an adult to whom they are connected. Make it clear (especially in an elementary setting or any setting where teachers only have one group of students to serve rather than multiple groups) that teachers should not simply take all of the cards of kids they teach this year. Instead, they should really focus on the criteria about students feeling connected. Reinforce that they are only to pick the students with whom the criteria are met, and reassure them that you and your leadership team will take care of any postcards that are left over.

Your staff will see immediately that some of their colleagues take a handful of cards while others stick to just a few. Again, this is a self-assessment of how they feel they are connecting to kids. Your whole group reflection comes when you see the cards that are left on the table. This is a tough moment, whether there are two or three cards or fifty cards left. No one likes to think that any one student does not have at least one adult who feels they know the student well. But the fact is, it happens. It's very likely that when folks take a look at the names on the cards they will either not recognize the name at all (especially in larger schools), or they will not be surprised by the names, recognizing some of these students as kids who seem to be "loners."

This stack of leftover cards becomes the data by which you measure your effectiveness as a group on the relationship front. If you have a collective commitment to building relationships with all kids, then this is the time to discuss how you will deliberately go about making this happen. In one school, for example, it was this exact type of data that helped steer the leadership team down a road toward incorporating an advisory model into the school schedule—a deliberate strategy used to ensure that every student was grouped with an adult with whom they could build a relationship over their three years in the school.

A wonderful side effect of this type of activity is how some members of your staff respond and step up. At our initial postcard writing, we had a couple of hundred kids (out of a school of about fifteen hundred) who did not have an adult identify as being connected to them. Our leadership team was prepared to write notes for these kids, but what we found is that a small group of our staff rallied, committed to ensuring that these kids got an extra-special note. They came around later, looking for the stack and going back through it again with the express purpose of beginning the process of getting to know some of these kids. This was one of those moments as a school leader when you just sit back and think, now that's why we are all here.

The last phase of this work to gauge your effectiveness with relationships is to, if you so desire, combine the two outcomes. Have the student surveys available to staff. Invite any who would like to, to bring their stack of post-cards and see, of the students they chose, how many of those students identified them as an adult they felt connected to; again a powerful point of reflection for any staff member brave enough to take the leap.

Now that you've established a data-based understanding of your school team's effectiveness with relationships in general, let's move the discussion back to the classroom. Each teacher now has a stronger sense of how they are perceived by students. Armed with this information, they can work toward adopting classroom management techniques that emphasize creating a positive classroom culture where every voice is valued.

As the leader, you are poised to tackle this work and create the opportunities for dialogue about what works and what doesn't work and any common protocols that the team may opt to use, even to showcase the staff who got particularly strong results from the assessment. Modeling the act of seeking expertise from among your team can ensure that any professional learning that occurs can be reinforced on a regular basis. Bear in mind that one important step in effective classroom management is the inclusion of student voices in the protocols and routines. We'll visit this topic in depth in chapter 7.

For now, our next step is to take a look at some scenarios that occur when effective strategies to avoid power struggles in the classroom are not in place. If you haven't already reviewed the lesson and its strategies from chapter 8, this is the time to do so. The model used in that chapter (listed here), as well as the strategies introduced, is applied to the vignettes shared in chapters 3 through 7:

- Opener/Setting the Stage (modify based on the information gained as a result of the brainstorming session)
- Pre-assessment/Scenario (insert selected vignettes here)
- The Learning
- The Practice
- Formative Assessment

THE PRACTICE

Following are a series of vignettes that can be incorporated into the primary lesson from chapter 8 and that are specifically designed to tackle the issue of power struggles in the classroom. After each vignette, an alternative approach is offered that directly addresses the specific vignette as well as, in some cases, the unintended consequences identified. You are encouraged to share these alternatives once the lesson from chapter 8 has been completed with staff.

Vignette I: The Behavior Contract (Elementary)

Mr. Thompson teaches third grade at a small, rural elementary school and has done so for many years. In general he is a likeable teacher, soft spoken, direct, and kind. Today has been a tough day. Stephen, a student who requires a behavior contract for day-to-day success, has not been responsive to the usual prompts and strategies.

Mr. Thompson is at his wit's end. After following all of the warning stages of the behavior contract with no success, Mr. Thompson snaps and approaches Stephen angrily. Stephen has refused to begin writing on the current assignment and is openly trying to distract the students closest to him.

Mr. Thompson stands over Stephen's desk and commands, "Stephen, that's it. Either start writing now or you're going to lose the opportunity to complete the assignment at all." This is a trigger for Stephen, much like any student, as the thought of failing scares him. Stephen responds by grabbing his paper and holding it to his chest. "No, I'll start," he says. He puts the paper back down and puts his head down on his desk. "You just lost it," Mr. Thompson says in a raised voice and then proceeds to grab the paper from under Stephen's head. "No," Stephen yells as he reaches to grab the paper back. A brief tug-of-war ensues over the paper until Mr. Thompson wrestles it loose and proceeds to ball it up, walk to the trash, and throw it in.

"Your bad choices are what got us here, Stephen. You need to think about that." Stephen, red faced and stuttering, puts his head back down on his desk. Mr. Thompson takes a seat at his desk, confident that this tough-love strategy will result in better cooperation in the future.

*(**Unintended consequence**: Several students in the class are shocked by Mr. Thompson's tone, especially since he is usually so calm. One young girl, Lisa, is particularly upset and almost in tears. When she arrives home that afternoon, she bursts into tears and tells the story to her mom. "Mr. Thompson isn't nice at all, Mom. He pretends to be nice but he's mean. We all know that Stephen has a special program, and Mr. Thompson being mean to him just makes it worse. What if he does that to me and tears up my paper if he thinks I am making a bad choice?" Lisa's mom makes a note to call Mr. Thompson the next day to share the impact of his actions on the other students.)*

Alternative Approach to Vignette I: The Behavior Contract (Elementary)

This vignette acknowledges that well-intentioned teachers can succumb to power struggles. As you begin this work with staff, it will be important to acknowledge that as important as working to eliminate power struggles is, it's equally important to honor the commitment to go back and address them when they have occurred despite our best efforts.

First let's address the power struggle as it played out. Of utmost importance is a teacher's ability to acknowledge in real time when he has reached a frustration level that threatens to spill over into the interaction with the student. What mechanisms does your school team have in place that can be employed when this happens? For example, is Mr. Thompson able to reach out and get classroom coverage for a few minutes to take a deep breath and maybe take a moment to strategize with a colleague on how to move forward with Stephen?

Another mechanism to have in place is the opportunity for Stephen to take some space in a neighboring classroom so that both he and the teacher can have a brief time-out. Your role is to ensure that your team has discussed these types of alternatives and is well versed in (a) what's available and (b) how to take advantage of the resource. Having this conversation early ensures that the resources are in place proactively, as opposed to waiting for the tough situations to occur and then simply reacting.

In this case, Mr. Thompson proceeds to interact with Stephen even in his heightened state of frustration. He has shifted into an "I'll teach you" mentality that is designed to demonstrate that he, the teacher, is in control. What he is likely not consciously acknowledging is that it is also demonstrating that he, the teacher, is the winner and Stephen, the student, is the loser. His thought is that by showing Stephen's who is boss, he will get Stephen to submit to his requests. In the long run we know that the teacher may get what he wants in the moment, for Stephen to stop distracting others. However, he gets this at great cost.

First, of course, Stephen is now completely eliminated from the learning process. He has no route by which to re-enter the learning process. Added to that is his utter humiliation in front of his peers. Humiliation can be a game changer for an indefinite period of time, depending on the person.

At an even more extreme level, Mr. Thompson escalated the power struggle from words only to words and physicality when he entered into the tug-of-war over the paper with Stephen. In this way, he insisted on not just verbal dominance but physical dominance over Stephen. This is frightening for any child, regardless of his demeanor, and is absolutely going to scare more students than just Stephen. Every student in that classroom took notice of this act and will internalize it as a part of their experience with Mr. Thompson as the school year progresses.

Regarding our strategies, Mr. Thompson has likely employed strategies similar to 1 through 3 (see chapter 8) just by virtue of implementing Stephen's behavior plan. These types of strategies are frequently found in such plans. At this point, then, he is best served by employing strategies 4 and 5. This is tough for a teacher, especially when the student is distracting others. That said, engaging the student when frustrated is going to have far more dire consequences than the student himself distracting his peers. Again, as your team moves forward, it will have the additional alternatives that you've agreed upon to get support.

For now, Mr. Thompson can walk away from the power struggle while letting Stephen know that they will pick up the matter later. This gives both him and Stephen a chance to cool off and think more clearly. Likewise, it ensures that the rest of the students are not witness to a side of Mr. Thompson they will not forget anytime soon, thereby avoiding the unintended consequence identified earlier.

As you counsel Mr. Thompson in the aftermath of this power struggle, it is imperative that you impress upon him the importance of circling back with Stephen and the entire class about what happened. Given that Mr. Thompson has likely received that call from Lisa's mom (and perhaps other concerned parents), he will be anxious to address the situation with his class. This is where your modeling of how you reflect on and "fix" your mistakes with staff will go a long way toward Mr. Thompson's feeling confident about doing the same.

Discuss with him how he plans to address the situation with the class. Emphasize the importance of being frank and simple about his frustration, his choices on how to handle his frustration, and what he now wishes he had done differently. Most critically, this is a chance for Mr. Thompson to invite the class, including Stephen, to brainstorm together ways they can all deal with frustration when it occurs in school so that they become a resource to one another. In this way the "I" versus "Them" mentality that was created with the power struggle can be cast aside and replaced with the "We" mentality that existed prior to the incident.

Vignette II: The Drill Sergeant (Middle School)

Mr. Lotus has just arrived as the new eighth-grade math teacher. In his interview, he impressed the panel with what appeared to be a positive outlook on kids and learning and a passion for going the distance to help every student succeed. Midway through the first quarter of school, the principal began getting reports from disgruntled parents about Mr. Lotus's demeanor toward students, with many parents citing examples of Mr. Lotus using physical punishments as a means to get students to succumb to his wishes.

The principal immediately began to investigate the situation by questioning students from a variety of Mr. Lotus's classes. She learned that Mr. Lotus had, in fact, employed a means of classroom management that included physical punishments. One prime example was Mr. Lotus's policy that students who failed to bring in homework were made to do push-ups in front of the class.

At first, students went along with it, thinking it was funny. It didn't take long, however, for Mr. Lotus's behavior to escalate when he realized students were treating the punishments as a joke. The situation came to a head during one class when a student laughed when told to do push-ups and refused to do them. Mr. Lotus continued to increase the number assigned until the student finally capitulated.

In addition to the physical punishment, the principal learned that students had become anxious about the class because they never knew what to expect from the teacher. Some days he appeared happy and accommodating, even going overboard to be solicitous with the students. Other days, with what appeared to be exactly the same circumstances, Mr. Lotus would be disgruntled and hostile from the moment students entered the room.

On these days, students noted that Mr. Lotus frequently engaged students in power struggles over the smallest of issues (i.e., leaving seats to sharpen pencils, requests to go to the bathroom, unwillingness to answer questions when called on, etc.). The constant extremes served to make the classroom a generally hostile environment. Learning was erratic at best.

*(**Unintended consequences:** In an effort to narrow the unintended consequences down to one, we will focus on Mr. Lotus's role on the Algebra 1 team. The team is working collaboratively to improve standardized test scores as a result of a slip in scores the previous year. They have been unaware of Mr. Lotus's classroom approach. Now they are scrambling to find coverage for Mr. Lotus's classes to support learning so that his students do not get so far behind that they cannot catch up.)*

Alternative Approach to Vignette II: The Drill Sergeant (Middle School)

As a school leader, this is the type of scenario that you strive to prevent. The hiring process itself is designed to "weed out" these types of personalities to ensure that the teacher/student relationship is positive and well-meaning. Unfortunately, as with any human endeavor, there are always going to be times when someone slips through.

In the case of Mr. Lotus, the entire hiring panel conveyed shock and surprise. There was absolutely no hint of this personality issue in his interview. This was confirmed further when the panel learned that two other schools had also made Mr. Lotus offers of employment. Clearly, he had fooled everyone.

When prevention fails, then you are left with fixing the problem that is created. Your direct observation of the teacher in the classroom setting via unannounced drop-ins will be a critical step. It is very likely that the teacher will be on his best behavior during these drop-ins. Perhaps he is aware that his techniques would be frowned upon and so he will avoid using them in front of another adult. On the other hand, it is possible that he believes his techniques are appropriate. He may defend them to you in follow-up conversations as an effective way to mold student behavior.

Ultimately it's that one-to-one conversation that will be the critical next step. Whether you witnessed behaviors of concern during your observation or not, you will be preparing your approach to how to coach Mr. Lotus in this situation. One note: Given the nature of the allegations, be sure to have contact with your human resources department every step of the way.

In large part, the primary intention of your conversation with Mr. Lotus will be to make your expectations about relationships with students clear. You'll share with him the allegations and, depending on whether he confirms them or not, be prepared to proceed in one of two ways:

1. If Mr. Lotus is open about his strategies, if he acknowledges the moodiness observed by students, and demonstrates a desire to im-

prove, then you can be in coaching mode. Your next step will be to work with him to identify an action plan that you will use together to restart his classroom-management approach. The steps included will vary, but will include having an honest conversation with his classes about their concerns, reassuring students that he understands why he must change his approach, and showing an honest effort on his part to do so.

You will closely monitor his actions as you demonstrate support for the students by addressing their concerns head-on and for the teacher by being there to ensure that his efforts are effective and to support him if they are not. Your next steps will involve ongoing monitoring, touching base with students, parents, and the teacher to get feedback, and a set schedule of follow-up coaching sessions with the teacher.

2. If Mr. Lotus denies the allegations or confirms the allegations, but denies that change is needed, then you have a very different problem to solve. In your initial conversation, you will work through a modified version of the lesson in chapter 8 to gauge Mr. Lotus's understanding of and agreement with this alternative approach. Can he see the negative impact of power struggles on student learning? If so, you can proceed in the coaching mode under very strict monitoring.

Of course, Mr. Lotus has to be willing to have the reflective conversation about his actions that we discussed above. If he is not willing to do this, then his commitment to eliminating power struggles and improving his classroom environment is not strong enough for him to proceed in the classroom.

This second approach becomes one where you must partner closely with your human resources department. It cannot be an option that you allow students to be subjected to the emotional stress that comes with dealing with an adult with extreme mood swings and a propensity to abuse what he considers a relationship of power and dominance.

Consider that, if Mr. Lotus is not immediately removed, you will have to work with your team to identify another adult to be present in his classrooms at all times. This is your only hope in the interim to ensure that: (a) students feel supported in that they are not left alone to be subjected to the teacher's behavior and (b) Mr. Lotus has another teacher to model the alternatives outlined in chapter 8, on the chance that he could be swayed to see things differently.

Vignette III: The Pushover (High School)

Mrs. Sanders's social studies classroom usually has a laid-back atmosphere. She is just two short years away from retirement and, of late, has taken the tactic that hers should be a class where students can discuss matters related to government and United States history without the pressure of grades. In this way, students complete enough simple assignments to earn a grade but otherwise spend most class blocks either watching history movies or engaged in discussion about current events.

Mrs. Sanders prides herself in having very few disciplinary issues and uses a collaborative method at the start of the year to create classroom rules with the students. That said, students understand that they can usually get away with most behaviors as long as they "kiss up" to Mrs. Sanders. In general, students looking for an easy ride love her class and see her as a bit of a pushover. Students who are excited to learn often are frustrated with the class and the teacher.

Today Mrs. Sanders is hosting yet another discussion day where students are expected to offer a current-event topic, provide a brief summary, and then offer their opinion. Other students are then permitted to ask questions and offer counter-perspectives. Janelle volunteers her article, a piece on gay marriage as the Supreme Court is considering it. After Janelle offers her summary, and her perspective—that the court should support gay marriage—Mrs. Sanders opens it up to questions.

Immediately, a peer in the back of the room, Jonathan, begins a tirade of anti-gay comments. It is his belief that gay marriage is a sin and that the court should not be involved at all as this is a question for the Bible, not the government. Jonathan's comments kick off a barrage of argumentative statements as students around the room take sides and the discussion becomes escalated very quickly.

Mrs. Sanders, meanwhile, is allowing the escalation to continue. She believes that this is all a part of the learning process and that students should be permitted to "debate" their beliefs. Although it is evident that emotions are taking over, Mrs. Sanders is still surprised when Jonathan jumps up from his desk and gets in Janelle's face. At this, Mrs. Sanders goes over to interject and finds that she has let the student power struggle go on too long and that neither student is backing down.

She insists that Jonathan return to his seat, but he refuses, lashing out at her instead for supporting the students who are pro-gay. Mrs. Sanders takes offense at Jonathan's tone and words and steps closer to him while ordering him in a loud voice to sit down. The power struggle that started between Janelle and Jonathan has now shifted to Jonathan and Mrs. Sanders.

The teacher continues to argue with Jonathan and at some point grabs his arm to guide him to his chair. Jonathan reacts by yelling, "Don't touch me. And don't pretend to be the teacher now when all you do is sit in the back of the room and do nothing or sleep all class."

At this point, Mrs. Sanders walks away to call for an administrator to have Jonathan escorted from the class. Jonathan storms out of the classroom instead and goes to the main office. When Mrs. Sanders follows up with the administrator later, she makes it clear that Jonathan's words and actions were inexcusable and she expects the administrator to "throw the book" at him.

(Unintended consequence: Mrs. Sanders's laisser-faire attitude toward the classroom has actually resulted in many students having little or no respect for her as a teacher. Several of them go to the office after class to speak with the assistant principal on Jonathan's behalf. Though they don't agree with his beliefs, they do think that the situation is a direct result of Mrs. Sanders's approach to the classroom and, therefore, that Jonathan should not be the only one to "get in trouble.")

Alternative Approach to Vignette III: The Pushover (High School)

This vignette is riddled with areas to be addressed—everything from the impact of an ineffective teacher on students, especially one being permitted to "coast" through the year, to discussions on sensitive topics being poorly monitored, to the specific power struggle that was a direct result of Mrs. Sanders's lack of action. Keeping true to our primary topic, we'll focus on the power struggle between the teacher and student and address the other areas as they pertain to it.

As the school leader, when you become aware of this scenario, you have some decisions to make about how to proceed. Will you use it as a catalyst to discuss larger-scale concerns you've had about Mrs. Sanders's performance, or will you focus only on the interaction with Jonathan? It stands to reason that you would address both the larger issues as well as the specific power struggle. Ideally, you will help Mrs. Sanders see that by making improvements in some of those larger areas, she might avoid a power struggle like this in the future.

Your initial conversation with Mrs. Sanders will be an opportunity to let her vent and run through her version of the incident. You'll express understanding and certainly support the notion that no one (student or otherwise) should speak to another person in our school this way. In this initial conversation you will assure Mrs. Sanders that you will address Jonathan appropriately and that his behavior will not be repeated. This is important, as she is not likely to "hear" anything else you have to say without this preliminary reassurance out of the way.

This is an opportunity for you to remind Mrs. Sanders of your agreed-upon expectations for everyone (adults and students alike) to treat one another with dignity and respect. You can gauge her understanding of the agreed-upon expectations as well as her sense of how well she thinks she adheres to the expectations. Once Mrs. Sanders has shared her version of the incident, you can ask her to go back through it, step-by-step and discuss what facets she felt she could have prevented if she had acted differently.

It's important to reiterate your mantra that "we cannot control others but, instead, can only control ourselves." Given that, what could she have changed about her own reaction to the scenario that might have ensured a more positive outcome? If Mrs. Sanders falters, you will provide guidance by steering her back to the professional learning on power struggles and the six strategies from chapter 8. From the moment she interjected herself into the power struggle between Janelle and Jonathan, Mrs. Sanders had the opportunity to deescalate the situation.

Did she approach the two in a nonthreatening and supportive manner? Did she make it clear that she wasn't there to pick sides but, instead, intended to bring the discussion back to a proper debate format? If Mrs. Sanders does not answer these questions accurately (in other words, if she perceives her actions as different from how the students perceived them), then you will have to enlighten her about how she was perceived.

You'll want to emphasize that though the perception may be different, it's critical that Mrs. Sanders be willing to acknowledge that the students' perception of the situation is just as important as the reality. This part of the conversation may be challenging but will be essential in order to proceed.

Once Mrs. Sanders is willing to consider the other perceptions, you can walk her through the six strategies and, together, agree on which would have been helpful here in diffusing the situation. It's likely that number 1, used very strategically, would be key. When she approached Jonathan he was already heated and emotional. His mindset at that point was not conducive to receiving demands from one more "combatant," as he was already in the defensive mode with Janelle.

Mrs. Sanders could have simply, calmly, stated her intention—that she needed to get the classroom discussion back on track so that everyone's opinions could be heard—perhaps even explained that at this point, no one was listening to anyone else, so Jonathan's points were not having the desired effect. Next, she could ask that he help her out by either returning to his seat or, if he needed a moment to gather himself, step into the hall and come back in when he was ready.

A key here is that the teacher understands that hostility only breeds more hostility. Approaching the student with a loud or angry or disrespectful tone will only set him on a more negative road, and by doing so, she will contribute to the situation escalating.

If strategy 1 does not serve to end the power struggle the first time, then Mrs. Sanders should continue to reiterate the choices while maintaining her calm demeanor. She'd want to check herself for strategy 2 as well to ensure that her words are not contributing to Jonathan's escalation. Giving him negative messages and ultimatums will not work, though they become tempting when the student doesn't respond immediately. Instead, the repeated effort to offer choices, more often than not, will result in interrupting the negative behavior. This interruption is what leads to the student beginning to calm down.

Once he is seated or out of the room, Mrs. Sanders then has the next decision to make: does she attempt to just move on with class as if the disruption did not occur, or does she acknowledge the incident and try to debrief with the group in an effort to mitigate future power struggles? This is a judgment call.

It's important for the teacher to be able to read the temperature of the room. If students are still emotional, it is best to simply acknowledge that things got out of hand, apologize for any contribution the teacher, as the adult, may have made to it, and reassure students that they will come back to it in the next class when everyone has had the chance to regroup. This both honors the students' input by letting them know they will have a voice in the debriefing and ensures that no additional flare-ups occur. Mrs. Sanders can then move on with class.

The delay in debriefing also has the added benefit of giving Mrs. Sanders the opportunity to debrief with a colleague first. Consulting with a mentor, supervisor, or other trusted colleague will ensure that Mrs. Sanders is think-ing about all angles and is better prepared to debrief with the students in a way that maintains everyone's dignity. A conversation with an administrator can be the opening for delving into Mrs. Sanders's general approach to the classroom, what works, what does not work, and how to provide her support in order to improve her effectiveness overall in the teaching and learning relationship.

This time lapse also gives Mrs. Sanders an opportunity to talk with Jona-than privately. It is understood that Mrs. Sanders will role-play this conversa-tion with an administrator first. In this conversation, she will work to better understand the nature of Jonathan's assertions about her as a teacher and to acknowledge them, however appropriate, based on the earlier conversation about her performance with the administrator.

This piece is necessary in order for her classroom environment to begin to become one that is more conducive to learning. The conversation with Jona-than means that the two of them are on the same page when she debriefs with the entire class, and Jonathan now becomes a partner in the effort to make the overall learning experience in Mrs. Sanders's classroom more positive, fo-cused, and more likely to result in improved student achievement.

Vignette IV: Oh Homework, My Homework (Middle School)

Ms. Tally is in her fourth year of teaching science to sixth graders at her suburban middle school. She is generally well regarded as hardworking and collaborative. This year, she has struggled with the school team's decision to begin a process to overhaul grading practices in an effort to move toward standards-based grading and to create more consistency with grading among teachers.

Though she was able to work with her sixth-grade science professional learning community (PLC) to agree on a common grade-book structure, one area where they cannot agree is homework. Ms. Tally believes strongly that homework is an essential part of the learning process. To that end, she has refused to embrace the idea of not counting homework in the grade book. Instead, she has compromised by significantly decreasing its' weight in the overall grading picture.

As Ms. Tally prepares for her first-period class, she is already dreading the arrival of Lindsey. Lindsey is a bright student who, according to Ms. Tally, is not motivated and doesn't work up to her potential. This is most evident in her frequent refusal to complete homework. More and more, first period feels like a battleground with Ms. Tally and Lindsey pitted against one another.

At the start of class, Ms. Tally directs students to take out their homework and put it on their desks for her to check. As she moves from student to student, she simply picks up each sheet to see that both sides have been completed. When Ms. Tally arrives at Lindsey's desk, she finds a half completed assignment. "Lindsey, you didn't finish your homework so you can't get credit." Lindsey, seemingly just waiting for the power struggle to begin, responds "That's not fair. I did part of it so I should get part credit." "You know my policy," Ms. Tally responds. "All or none." "That doesn't make any sense," Lindsey replies, "all you're doing is checking it off. You're not even checking to see if anyone got the answers right."

Ms. Tally responds firmly, "Lindsey, I'm not going to argue with you" and moves on to the next student. Lindsey's agitation increases as she looks around and sees, once again, that all eyes are on her. Some students are laughing and whispering while others are just shrugging as if to say, "Nothing you can do about it."

Lindsey calls out to Ms. Tally again. "Ms. Tally I still don't think it's fair that I'm not getting any credit. If you'd look at my sheet you'd see that at least my answers are correct and at least I did my own work. I know you know some kids copy each other's work in the locker area in the mornings, and you just give them credit anyway without doing anything to stop it. I don't get it. What's the point if we're not going to check it and make sure we got things right."

Ms. Tally takes the bait and launches into her usual explanation about the importance of practice and of learning time management and taking responsibility as a learner. Lindsey continues to counter with assertions about how practice doesn't work if there is no review and you don't know what you did right or wrong. This back and forth sparring continues as Ms. Tally circulates in the room and continues to check homework.

Eventually, other students begin to grumble and comment under their breath in agreement with Lindsey. Ms. Tally's patience begins to wear thin. Her frustration is magnified by the fact that no one is working on their warm-up problem because they are distracted by the debate. She finally lashes out at the whole class. "Fine, if you don't like the homework policy then tell me why. For homework tonight each of you is to write a five-hundred-word essay on why homework is important. I want you to really think about it and come up with at least one reason. No exceptions."

(Unintended Consequence: Though Ms. Tally sees her assignment as an act of collaboration, the students are well beyond that. Given that she created the policy without their voice and has battled all year with various students about it, most see the assignment as punishment and a way to warn them to not argue in the future. This doesn't bode well for her ongoing relationships.)

Alternative Approach to Vignette IV: Oh Homework, My Homework (Middle School)

The fact is, homework is a scary word these days. And of course you can't talk about homework without talking about grading in general (insert shudder here). Grading is a hotbed of conflict and power struggles both between adults and kids as well as between adults. We could have easily added a grading vignette to almost every chapter of this book, given the pervasive problems caused by our different philosophies and beliefs about it.

As much as we'd love to tackle grading here, it is not our primary focus. Perhaps it can be the topic of the next edition of this book. The scenario is fairly classic in that it plays out in classrooms and schools all over and crosses all geographic, socioeconomic, and cultural lines. Grading is always reflective of our core beliefs about education and, as such, becomes a tough place to compromise.

For now, let's address the issues raised around homework in this vignette that led to the power struggle between Ms. Tally and Lindsey. You became aware of this situation when you happened to stop by Ms. Tally's room to check in informally. You asked how she was and she launched into a description of the power struggle that had occurred the day before. It is clear that she felt Lindsey was rude to question her and that assigning the class an essay was a great way to curb future arguments.

Your next step is to pause and assure Ms. Tally that you totally understand why she was upset by the incident. No one likes to be questioned and it's always uncomfortable to feel like you are on the defense. Additionally, you know that Lindsey is known for her lack of effort and that Ms. Tally is not the only teacher who has become frustrated by her laisser-faire attitude. By demonstrating understanding of her plight, you gain Ms. Tally's trust that you are looking out for her—that's a delicate balance as you want to show support while not appearing to give approval of the grading policy and her actions themselves.

Turns out you are well aware of Ms. Tally's grading system because she has been a holdout with the science team. You see this as a prime opportunity to address grading via the power struggle incident. That said, you recognize that the grading conversation is a long one, and you don't want to miss the opportunity to model the learning about power struggles, either. To that end, you bring Ms. Tally back to the professional learning on power struggles.

Be sure to start by asking her if she sees the incident as a power struggle. As always, if she doesn't, then you have to tackle that first. To do so, you simply point out the conditions discussed in the power struggle lesson. Were both people (Ms. Tally and Lindsey) intent on winning the argument? Were both refusing to listen with reason to the other's responses? Did Ms. Tally notice that Lindsey's and, eventually Ms. Tally's as well, commitment to winning increased when she realized there was an audience?

Once Ms. Tally recognizes that she was engaged in the power struggle, you'll want to remind her of our strategies. Ask her to identify which, if any, of the strategies she felt she used. Ms. Tally might assert that she used strategy 2 because she didn't use negative words. You can acknowledge that and also acknowledge that, clearly, strategy 2 was not enough to prevent the power struggle. Now you can turn it to what she might do differently in the future.

Encourage Ms. Tally to consider strategy 4 in the future. One of Lindsey's concerns seems to be that she didn't think Ms. Tally was listening to her (now, in the mind of a pre-teen that's partly because listening to me equals doing what I want, so we have to allow for that). If Ms. Tally offered the option to delay the discussion until later in class when they could speak privately in the hallway, then the escalation that occurred would have been minimized.

Likewise, a delay would have given Ms. Tally a chance to regroup rather than letting her frustration grow until she handed out a group consequence. And, yes, part of your responsibility here is to help Ms. Tally see that the essay assignment was absolutely a punishment, whether she realized it in the moment or not. Since it's too late for Ms. Tally to cancel the assignment, a strong teachable-moment move would be to ask Ms. Tally to be sure to schedule a time to talk with you later in the week so that she can summarize the students' responses. This ensures that she takes the step of reading and absorbing the student feedback, versus simply using it as one more check-off homework assignment.

Once you feel that you've addressed the power struggle itself, you can move on to discussing how these type of power struggles are often rooted in beliefs about grading. You start by asking Ms. Tally to remind you about the details of her homework policy. She sees it as simply that if you finish the entire assignment, you get a check in her book; if you don't complete the entire assignment, you do not get the check. At the end of the quarter, a student's percentage of checks earned is entered as a homework grade in her book.

Now that Ms. Tally has shared the nuances of her homework policy you shift into asking clarifying questions. You might simply start with, "Tell me the outcome you are looking for by using your homework policy." This may be confusing for her—"what you do mean by outcome?"; she may err on the side of throwing out the "they need to learn responsibility" mantra, or she may even earnestly reply that she "grades" homework as a way of ensuring that students practice the learning. Let's assume the best and go with the third response. Ms. Tally genuinely believes that by checking for completion, she is ensuring good practice at home.

"Let's delve into that," you respond. "How do you know if completing the homework you assign actually results in greater learning? Do you use a formative assessment in your warm-up, for example, to assess this, or do you have students check their answers for accuracy?" If Ms. Tally is truly committed to homework being a part of the learning process, then she will find a way to answer this question with what she believes is sound reasoning.

This becomes a defining moment, then, because the points you counter with are probably going to sound a lot like the points that Lindsey threw out to her, because Lindsey's points weren't, well, wrong. Her presentation and timing were way off, but her points were valid (see the scenario in chapter 7 with the student side of this vignette). This, friends, is what we call a "courageous conversation."

"OK, so you shared that Lindsey said that students copy each other's homework. Do you believe that happens?" Ms. Tally will likely pause on this one. Truth is, many teachers see students sitting by their lockers and sharing work. Heretofore, no one interjects. It's easier to walk on by and assume they're not actually copying or otherwise cheating. "Well, I mean it's probably likely that that happens sometimes. I can't really control that. All I know is that if they come to class with a completed assignment, then they get the credit."

Carefully, you can pretend to think out loud: "You know, I'm guessing it happens a lot. This conversation is making me realize we should bring this up with our honor code committee. For now, though, can we agree that ignoring the practice and giving credit no matter what might be confusing for kids? What do you think your students believe is the purpose of homework in your class?"

Ultimately, what you are creating is an opportunity to demonstrate that there are multiple beliefs about grading and that it's important that each of us as educators constantly reflect on our beliefs and processes as a way of ensuring that they don't get outdated and counterproductive. By continuing to ask probing questions, you are leading Ms. Tally down a path of reflection that can only result in growth.

This is just the beginning of a hard conversation with just one teacher in your school. Your key role in this conversation is inquiry, seeking to understand. Of course you have your own beliefs about grading, but you'll also have to recognize that every educator does, and to simply approach others with an "I hear you but this is my way" attitude will make the grading conversation a very slippery slope. Instead, by seeking to understand, and combining that with providing frequent, ongoing access to best-practice research, you will be better primed to begin the grading evolution in your school. Perhaps we'll make grading the next iteration of this book.

WRAP-UP

Power struggles, and the devastating tangential areas to which they can lead in the classroom, are undoubtedly a foundational flaw to effective classroom management. When power struggles go unchecked and are allowed to exist in the classroom, it becomes obvious that student learning is taking a backseat to the adult power play. This alone ensures that students are getting the message loud and clear that they have no power, no voice, and no individual or collective value. It becomes the leader's role, then, to know both what is or is not happening and to take a stand for the sake of each individual affected daily by the culture of the school.

Chapter Four

From Start to Finish

Power Struggles That Impact Student Learning
throughout the Day

The school day starts for kids the moment they exit their home in the morning on the way to school. Their involvement with school staff can begin as early as the moment they set foot on the school bus. From there they begin a day of innumerable interactions with adults in the school environment, each of which has its impact on the students' overall availability for learning.

Relationships are at the core of student success, and, as a result, each interaction students have during the school day either positively or negatively impacts their ability to learn. Yes, many of these interactions will be with peers, and any school leader can speak for days about the impact of peer drama on learning. But our focus in this chapter is on adults, so we will leave that for now and come back to it in chapter 7. Likewise, in chapter 7 we will address how to guide students in handling power struggles with adults of all titles and positions.

At the heart of the instructional approach of this book is the lesson on power struggles that is outlined in chapter 8. This basic lesson structure and the strategies used in it remain the same across all populations. What varies, then, is the *nuance* of how an adult's title or role impacts her interactions with students.

Keep in mind, also, that sometimes the adult's title puts her in a unique position to be treated differently by the student. This, of course, then plays into how the power struggle may erupt. Additionally, the unintended consequences of these confrontations can vary based on titles and, therefore, must be addressed individually.

IT STARTS WITH YOU: THE LEARNING

As a school leader, a great starting place is to work with your leadership team to identify all of the various "positions" held by adults in your building. There is an assumption that your leadership team is made up of staff from all realms, to include certified and classified. If not, be sure that the group tackling this issue does have this level of representation. It does no one any good to discuss a problem with no key representatives from the core group present and contributing to the discussion. At its core, this is a brainstorming session. Be sure to acknowledge, especially given the personal and sensitive nature of this discussion, the rules for brainstorming:

- no negativity or criticism—all ideas are valid at this stage;
- everyone must contribute;
- no distractions—that means put away all electronic devices and resort to good old-fashioned hand scripting of notes;
- all ideas, the crazier or more outlandish the better, can help improve the thinking of the group;
- take turns talking and rein in the over talkers—use a timing system if necessary;
- resist tangents and storytelling.

   Back to your list; remember to include in your list both part-time and full-time employees, adults who are assigned to your building but who come and go (school psychologists, probation officers, etc.), and nonemployees like volunteers. Once the list is compiled, begin to brainstorm examples of power struggles that members of your team have actually observed or have been made aware of—the goal here is to create a list of examples that touches on each and every position the team listed. Examples in hand, now share the outcomes.

   How was each power struggle resolved? Was there a clear-cut "winner" and "loser?" Was there an audience? If so, what may have been some unintended consequences based on the audience? What, if any, role did you feel that the title of the adult played in how the student responded? So far, you have a document that may look as simple as Table 4.1.

   The completion of this brainstorming session is critical to determining how to approach training with all of these adults. Do not be surprised if you start to see some trends. Certainly, despite titles, you will find that the adults in your building are on a spectrum with respect to how they respond to power struggles with students. Despite their titles, some will be adept at avoiding power struggles and at naturally employing some or all of the strategies outlined in our primary lesson. Others, however, will struggle, and still oth-

Table 4.1.

Position	Example of PS	Outcome	Unintended Consequence	Role that Title Played in Student Response
1)	1)	1)	1)	1)
2)	2)	2)	2)	2)

ers will be quick to engage in the power struggle with a belief that it is as simple as, "I'm the adult and therefore you must respect me."

The brainstorming session is likely to dredge up the delicate topic of the role of noncertified staff and the fact that oftentimes it is adults in these positions who feel disenfranchised in a poor school culture. It is often these very adults who, if not addressed deliberately by the school leader, feel that they have no voice and that their work is undervalued. This is important to acknowledge because if this is true in your school, then this inherent problem has to be addressed either along with the power struggles issue or before it can even be tackled.

Human nature dictates that if people feel un-empowered, then they are more likely to try to exert power over others who they feel are under their control. The result can be a higher frequency of incidents of power struggles between noncertified staff and students and a greater need for professional development.

Let's explore this possibility for a moment. If you have determined that this is true of your noncertified staff (and if you are unsure, it likely means it is true; frankly, if it is not true, then you will be certain about that because you will be confident in the relationships you have built with this sector of your school team), what steps will you take to begin to turn the tide?

There is nothing more powerful then open, honest conversation. Here are some key questions to jumpstart your thinking:

- Do you create regular opportunities for your cafeteria staff, your custodians, your teaching assistants, and so on to meet with you to discuss concerns?
- Do you make it a point to observe them in action and comment on their performance?
- Do these staff members, like others, have a direct link to you, or are they forced to go through someone else (an administrative assistant, for example) to see you?
- Do you include these staff members in regular, consistent school communications (i.e., weekly e-mailed newsletters), or are they inadvertently left out due to a lack of access?

If you find yourself answering *no* to two or more of these questions, then you likely have a problem. A simple way to start addressing the problem is by changing your leadership behavior in a way that allows you to answer *yes* to these questions. Again, start with an honest conversation. An effective school leader is brave enough to sit with his or her staff and discuss their concerns without giving in to the instinct to defend past behaviors. An effective school leader is one who can acknowledge an area of weakness and speak openly about both a desire to improve and a willingness to collaborate in doing so.

THE PRACTICE

You must be aware of and in tune with the critical impact that every adult in the school has on every student. It is not enough to train teachers on how to manage and eliminate power struggles; you must train each and every staff member, keeping in mind that their specific roles have an impact on both how they will approach their interactions with students and how comfortable they will be in learning how to diffuse power struggles.

Note that one additional component for this group of staff is the acknowledgment that they may be treated differently by some students simply because those students feel the staff members are inferior, based on their position. This is an unsavory topic but a brutally honest possibility. This is where your leadership belief that each person, despite title, age, role, status, and so on, deserves to have his or her dignity maintained by being treated respectfully becomes paramount to building a positive school culture. If you are being clear about this belief, making it a part of every message, sending it to every person in your school—staff and students alike—then the issue of position and title becomes one that is more easily overcome.

Vignette I: The Bus

It's Friday morning and Vivian climbs onto the bus after arguing with her mom about going to the game later that night. As she climbs the steps, the bus driver, Mr. Thomas, stops her, holds up the trashcan and orders her to spit out her gum. Vivian knows there is a no-gum rule on the bus, but ignores Mr. Thomas and tries to walk past him.

Mr. Thomas holds up an arm, blocking her path, and Vivian snaps, "I'm not chewing gum." Mr. Thomas responds with "either spit out the gum or get off of the bus. You know the rules." Vivian begrudgingly spits out her gum and mutters, "Good morning to you, too" as she continues down the aisle.

*(**Unintended consequence:** Just a few seats back is Jessica, a freshman who tends to be shy and quiet, especially around adults. After watching the*

confrontation, Jessica sends a quick text: "Mom, I don't want to ride the bus anymore, can you drive me to school tomorrow?")

Alternative Approach to Vignette I: The Bus

It is a great reminder for all school staff that, except in situations of great safety concerns, addressing students in a way that maintains their dignity is always an expectation. To that end, Mr. Thomas will gain a lot of ground by asking Vivian to spit out her gum versus ordering her to do so; yes, even if this is the hundredth time. The mantra "every day is a new day" may sound clichéd, but it is ever so true in the school setting. Vivian likely got on the bus looking for a fight, given the earlier problem with her mom. Mr. Thomas could not have known she was already in a bad mood.

The unknown is exactly why it is so important to begin each interaction with a positive tone. Simply stated, you can never know what baggage the person you are faced with is carrying around, so a positive approach will ensure that you do not do anything deliberately to add to that baggage. If Vivian does not respond by granting Mr. Thomas's request, then he is best served by letting her pass (strategy 4). He has made his point by addressing the rule violation (other students will note this), and he can come back to Vivian later.

An ideal time to follow up is that afternoon. Mr. Thomas can make a point of standing outside of the bus and greeting students as they board for the ride home. In this way, he can ask Vivian to step aside for a private conversation when she approaches. Vivian has now had time to move on from the morning's negativity and will more likely be in a frame of mind to actually discuss Mr. Thomas's concern.

Mr. Thomas can reiterate the rule and ask for her help in adhering to it. He may even make a point of sharing that when gum is spit out on the bus, he is responsible for cleaning it up (thereby helping Vivian better understand why the rule exists in the first place—strategy 3). This is designed to appeal to Vivian in hopes that she will not want to be responsible for creating more work for Mr. Thomas, whom she generally likes.

By choosing this route, Mr. Thomas also ensures that no other students on the bus start their day having witnessed a confrontation and that all students continue to see the bus as a positive, safe option for travel to school. Jessica now has no reason to text her mom and the unintended consequence, by extension, of creating a larger strain on the already overused parent drop-off is avoided.

Vignette II: The Main Office

It's the last day for students to buy tickets for the Homecoming dance and Alejandro enters the front office because he has just learned that he needs a special form for his girlfriend (who attends a neighboring high school) to attend the dance with him. Alejandro is new to the school and is still becoming familiar with school policies. The office is chaotic and filled with other students looking for assistance on a variety of topics. Some students are also inquiring about Homecoming tickets, others are signing in late to school, while still others are looking for help with jammed lockers.

It's a busy morning. Though Alejandro waits patiently, when he is finally greeted by the administrative assistant, he is quickly faced with a frustrated adult when the secretary, Mrs. DeAngelo, realizes what he needs. "You cannot get the form today because it has to be signed by your girlfriend's principal," she snaps. Alejandro attempts to explain that he is new and was unaware and is hoping the form can be faxed to her school. Mrs. DeAngelo is unwavering. "No exceptions, if we did that for every student we'd be faxing forms all day."

Alejandro moves from being distraught at the idea of not having a date for Homecoming to being angry that Mrs. DeAngelo won't discuss a compromise. "I don't get it, why won't you help me?" he asks. Mrs. DeAngelo dismisses his plea and, in a louder voice intended to dissuade others in line with the same request replies, "you've heard the announcements and you shouldn't have waited until the last day. We're done here." Interestingly enough, Mrs. DeAngelo's presumption is that every teacher provides access to the live morning announcements, which is not always the case.

*(**Unintended consequence:** In the midst of the crowd of students is Jaylen—she came to the office today to tell someone that she has smelled pot in the girls' bathroom on the first floor for the last few mornings. It bothers her, and she is worried that students may be going to class high. After witnessing Mrs. DeAngelo's response to Alejandro, Jaylen quietly leaves the office without reporting anything.)*

Alternative Approach to Vignette II: The Main Office

The scene described here is not unusual, especially given the heavy load of customer support a school's main office team often carries. The solution to Vignette II, quite frankly, harkens all of the way back to hiring decisions for this team. It is critical that you put the characteristic of "passionate to support kids" above all others when hiring the team in the main office.

Unfortunately, you often inherit these staff members, in which case establishing a hard and fast set of expectations for this team is imperative to building or repairing a school culture. It is a common notion among educators that you can "feel" a school's culture simply by walking into its main office; this notion is often totally accurate.

First and foremost, you will need to better understand why Mrs. DeAngelo is so quickly frustrated by Alejandro's request. Is this personal? In other words, is she simply having a bad day? Is this a reoccurring problem that has not been addressed by the leadership team despite her requests? Her response appears unreasonable on the surface, and it is important to determine what is behind it in order to garner a change of behavior in future situations.

Regardless of her motivation, Mrs. DeAngelo needs alternatives. One solution is to encourage staff members to take a break when they feel themselves being short with a student. Asking another staff person to jump in is not a sign of weakness but, instead, is a sign of a staff member wanting to ensure that every student is treated respectfully. Another solution, in the case where multiple students have the same request, and the staff person feels that there is no way to get all requests met, is to have a member of the leadership team available for extra support.

On the one hand, Mrs. DeAngelo feels she is in the right because the team has agreed that they will not succumb to the pressure to jump through hoops (i.e., fax forms to various schools for students) when students have waited until the last minute to follow procedures. On the other hand, there has to be a common understanding that there are always exceptions to the rule—especially in schools, since your target audience is children.

Having an administrator assigned to addressing these situations when they come up both preserves Mrs. DeAngelo's ability to stick to the rules while also acknowledging that staff has to be able to distinguish between those students who knew the procedure and procrastinated and those students who simply did not know the proper procedure.

Regardless of the solution that is most appropriate for your setting, Mrs. DeAngelo can take some steps of her own to avoid the confrontation. First, help instill some calm in the office by asking students to wait outside in the hall area until they are called in—the chaos that can be created by a crowd of needy students all confined to one space can in and of itself cause a negative vibe that can foster negative interactions. Next, use this new climate of calm to address each student individually and, to some degree, privately.

In this case, Mrs. DeAngelo may then feel more confident about making an exception for Alejandro upon taking the time to realize he is new to the school and really did not know better. He is exactly the reason there are exceptions to the rules. If she feels that an exception is not warranted, this environment also gives her an opportunity to problem solve with Alejandro (Does he have a parent who can pick up the form and take it to the school? Can he take a picture of the form and send it to his girlfriend to print out and get signed at her school?) and/or to at least acknowledge his sense of disappointment without being dismissive. This approaches ensures that Alejandro maintains his dignity even if he doesn't get what he wants.

Let's not forget the unintended consequence—Jaylen and her concern about marijuana use in the girls' bathroom. By working through the issue with Alejandro in a supportive way, Mrs. DeAngelo fosters a sense of support and collaboration among the office team that will be seen by students like Jaylen as an indicator that this is a safe place to come with concerns. Jaylen now has no reservations about making her report and possibly making a major contribution to solve the problem and help keep her peers safe.

Vignette III: The Instructional Assistant

Ms. Rubio has been a special education teaching assistant for two years. She reports directly to a special education program manager and her daily assignments change frequently. She often finds herself working in new classrooms with a variety of students—some disabled and others not disabled. It is sometimes challenging for her to ascertain where the line of authority stands.

Today Ms. Rubio finds herself assigned to offering one-to-one support to a student with a behavioral disability in the context of a general education geometry class. Immediately upon entering the classroom, Ms. Rubio finds her student, Melvin, engaged in a power struggle with the geometry teacher.

The teacher is pushing Melvin because, once again, he has come unprepared to class. Melvin wants a pass to his locker, while the teacher is standing fast that she will not issue him a pass as a consequence for his repeatedly coming unprepared. Melvin is beginning to escalate the power struggle, raising his voice and insisting on leaving the classroom. The teacher, in kind, is raising her voice and tells Melvin, "This is your fault, you'll just have to take the zero."

The reference to a potential poor grade is a known trigger for Melvin, as shown in his behavior plan, and Ms. Rubio knows that the power struggle is about to escalate even further. Though she is familiar with Melvin's behavior plan and knows how to intervene, she is unsure of how the teacher will respond if she interjects herself into the conversation.

*(**Unintended consequence:** Marissa, a nondisabled peer in the geometry class, has a positive rapport with the geometry teacher and is startled by the teacher's response to Melvin. The teacher has always shown leniency to her in turning in late assignments and Marissa questions why the rules are different for Melvin. Likewise, she can see that Ms. Rubio is uncomfortable with the interaction and wonders why she is not intervening on Melvin's behalf. "Ms. Rubio definitely doesn't have Melvin's back," she mumbles to another student sitting close by.)*

Alternative Approach to Vignette III: The Instructional Assistant

Let's begin with a disclaimer. Admittedly, this power struggle is as much about the two adults as it is about the student and adults. I've placed it in chapter 4, however, because it is a strong example of the types of power struggles that can influence a student's day. That said, we'll delve into the adult piece as well as how to diffuse the power struggle between the student and general education teacher.

Vignette III spotlights a typical power struggle between teacher and student in the classroom (addressed more thoroughly in chapter 3 so we will not address it here) as well as the struggle that arises when the adults in a situation are at odds with how to address the student. The struggle that can erupt between the adults in this scenario can have vast effects—either positive or negative.

As Ms. Rubio enters the classroom, she is thrust into what appears to be a lose-lose situation. If she interjects, she risks having the geometry teacher seeing her as "siding" with the student and undermining her authority in the classroom. If she does nothing, she risks the power struggle between teacher and student escalating as well as the onlooker students (i.e., Marissa) feeling that this has become an "us" (adults) versus "them" (students) culture.

It cannot be stressed enough how frequently this type of scenario is likely to unfold in a typical school day and, thus, how imperative it is for you to address this head-on. Pretending or hoping that this will not happen is a mistake. Much of the adult issues can be addressed by simply running through vignettes like this with adult teams and agreeing beforehand on how each will respond. In the case of Ms. Rubio and this teacher, they are not actually scheduled together. So, then, what is the expressed expectation that you as the school leader have established?

This brings us back to our lesson in chapter 8. When the lesson is conducted with all staff, it ensures that these situations are addressed similarly across the school and that both staff members in this vignette feel empowered to be a part of the solution. Imagine the powerful dialogue that will come from the lesson as solutions are brainstormed by a group of participants who represent all potential "players" in the scenarios. In this instance, both the teachers and teacher assistants can share with each other how they feel each should respond in order to come to an agreed-upon set of expectations.

Given the six strategies outlined in the chapter 8 lesson, Ms. Rubio has multiple options at her disposal. First and foremost, as a result of the lesson, she understands that there is a school-wide expectation that she intercede and that this expectation is set despite titles and roles. This helps her to feel empowered to take action. Ms. Rubio might enter the conversation using strategy 3—show understanding that you don't have to agree with the rule to follow it.

Given her knowledge of Melvin's behavior plan, she might simply say, "Excuse me, Melvin, I get that you're upset that you can't go to your locker and that you feel like it's no big deal for the geometry teacher to let you go. But have you thought about what would happen if every student every day didn't bring their materials and that every class started with everyone leaving to go to their lockers? Wouldn't that waste a lot of time and make things chaotic? I feel the same way when I leave my planning book at home—seems like I should just be able to go back and get it, but I can't leave school. It's really frustrating. I don't agree with the rule, but I know it's important to follow. Does that make sense?"

The idea is to distract Melvin's attention from the geometry teacher, giving her time to take a deep breath and regroup and hopefully getting Melvin to move on to strategizing about how to proceed without his materials. This strategy allows both the geometry teacher and Melvin a chance to back away from the power struggle while saving face and moves the conversation into the problem-solving phase.

If Melvin doesn't respond as hoped (and let's face it, that is often what happens, especially with students with significant behavioral disabilities), Ms. Rubio could then employ strategy 1—offer choices. "Melvin I can see you are still trying to argue with the geometry teacher. Why don't we step outside of the classroom for a moment to talk about what choices you have right now, because you do have choices."

Again, this strategy allows both student and teacher to maintain their dignity while moving the conversation to a problem-solving phase. Ms. Rubio can see that, more than anything, the teacher and student need some time apart. With both strategies, it is important that the teacher understand, as a result of the prior professional development, that it is appropriate to respect the assistant's attempt to interject and deescalate the power struggle. This is where the teacher models the concept that roles and titles are irrelevant and that we are all a part of the same team here to do the same work.

An important next step with this scenario is for the teaching assistant to feel empowered to circle back with the teacher later. The discussion should include a review of Melvin's behavior plan and a brief brainstorming session on how to avoid entering the power struggle with Melvin in the future. The sophisticated skill here is to not fall back on what the student needs to do different but, instead, to focus on what the teacher can control—herself—and reflect on the six strategies you've agreed to use as a school team and which she will employ in the future.

When this is done privately, it ensures growth on the part of both adults as well as dignity staying intact. This also seems like a great time to mention that these types of incidents and discussions should be kept confidential. It should go without saying, but frankly it doesn't, that Ms. Rubio would not discuss the situation with colleagues (save for an administrator or mentor from whom she is seeking guidance) as these types of conversations only feed a culture of rumors and negativity.

Circling back, let's think about how the use of these strategies then impact the unintended consequence. When these strategies are employed, the audience of onlookers (in this case, the entire geometry class) is now privy to both how to get out of a power struggle effectively and how to assist a peer in getting out of a power struggle. The rapport that the geometry teacher has built with students remains intact and students have confirmed for them that teachers and students are partners in learning.

Vignette IV: The Coach

The Varsity Girls' Softball team is district champion two years running, and the current senior class members are among the elite. The spring season has just begun, and the head coach, Coach Wilkins, has coached the team for seven years. Though she has coached this year's seniors for their entire high school career, she has been disappointed to find that the start of this season has been riddled with drama and mean-spiritedness among the players. The negativity appears to be led by her seniors.

Coach Wilkins has attempted to correct the behavior only to be met with resistance from the team leaders to the point of the team captains showing outright defiance to her instructions. In a recent conversation, Coach Wilkins confronted the captains about allegations of hazing of younger players. The captains' response was simply the message that this is their team, they are the champions, and the coach should let them lead in their own way. They accused Coach Wilkins of micro-managing the team and catering to the younger players.

The struggle for power has recently been made worse by an e-mail from the parents of the two captains. The e-mail was sent to the athletic director and included allegations against the coach of player mistreatment and a call for the coach's dismissal. The athletic director, Mr. Relm, is faced with mediating among all parties in an effort to right the balance of power and support the effort to get the team back on track. Mr. Relm calls a meeting with the parents of the two captains, the captains themselves, and the coach. In it he makes it clear that he supports the coach, that her word is final and that if the captains do not like it, they can certainly leave the team.

(Unintended consequence: Word quickly gets around to the athletic boosters association about the softball meeting. Though they support the athletic director's commitment to the coach and her efforts to eliminate the mean-spiritedness, Ms. Johnson and Mr. Waer, two of the booster club officers, are concerned about Mr. Relm's seeming dismissal of the voice of the parents. They share their concern with other booster parents and animosity begins to grow against the athletic director.)

Alternative Approach to Vignette IV: The Coach

For any school with an athletic program, the role of the coach is a big one in the lives of your young people. Whether the coach is a member of your staff or someone who just joins you for athletics, her impact on the students on her team absolutely crosses over into the classroom in negative and positive ways. In this scenario, the power struggle begins with the coach and team captains but then expands to include coach and parents as well as the parents and athletic director.

In the context of the lesson from chapter 8, the coach in this scenario could employ strategies 1 and 2 early on. Her primary goal is to stop the negativity and hazing among players (operating on the assumption that all of these allegations are true). She would, for example, outline the specific behaviors of concerns and give the captains an opportunity to explain their behavior.

Next she would demonstrate how the safety concerns raised violate school policy and offer the choices of ceasing the behavior, providing a team-bonding activity to put the team on a more positive track, or having the behavior reported to the athletic director if the captains refuse to cease. This in and of itself could lead to quick resolution. If strategies 1 and 2 do not work, given the student safety issues involved, the next step is to transition the dialogue from coach and athletes to athletes and athletic director as a disciplinary concern.

By allowing the dialogue to continue at the coach/athlete level, the coach is entering into the power struggle and extending the negative behavior. It becomes increasingly difficult to maintain dignity on the part of the coach and captains when there is a prolonged "tit for tat" conversation occurring over a short period of time. One additional strategy the coach might employ is to bring the entire team together to discuss concerns.

When handled effectively, this type of group conversation can both resolve the issues at hand, hazing and negativity toward younger players, and foster a greater sense of team among the players. That said, if handled ineffectively, this type of conversation could lead to more dissension and a fear on the part of some to speak up because of the possibility of retribution later. A coach's ability to lead in this type of scenario becomes an inherent part of the hiring process, a quality that is sought after when coaches are hired.

If the scenario extends to the point of involvement of both parents and the athletic director, then it is important that you as the school leader are offering a guiding hand in how to proceed. Though power struggles with parents are addressed at length in chapter 5, suffice it to say that in any discussion, all stakeholders must be made to feel valued and heard. Setting up a "winners" and "losers" scenario (like the one in this vignette) will only breed a larger power struggle. Just as the unintentional consequence suggests, what started out as a power struggle on one team can now grow into an issue that extends across the entire athletic program.

Vignette V: The Testing Coordinator

Mr. Foley is the testing coordinator at an elementary school. His role requires him to work among multiple school sites and, therefore, on three different school teams. Mr. Foley's role is unique in that the students recognize him as a regular face but don't see him often enough to fully understand what he does.

It's May and the testing season is in full swing. Mr. Foley is present almost every day and is primarily responsible for ensuring that testing begins and ends on time, testing guidelines are adhered to by school staff, and an appropriate testing environment is maintained at all times.

This Wednesday morning, third graders are engaged in math standardized testing while the rest of the school is carrying on a regular school day schedule. Mr. Foley has designated one part of the building as the testing zone and has asked that specific guidelines be followed to ensure that testing is not disrupted. These guidelines include no announcements via the intercom, no students permitted in the hallways, and so on. About halfway through the testing block, Sheila, a fourth grader, is given permission to go to the bathroom by her teacher.

Though her classroom is not in the designated testing area, Sheila opts to cut through there in order to swing by her friend's classroom to wave hello on her way. As she pauses in front of the classroom and attempts to get her friend's attention, Mr. Foley comes down the hall. He immediately calls out to Sheila, "Young lady, you are not supposed to be here." Sheila responds with a brief "OK, I'm going," but hesitates in one last attempt to say hello to her friend. Mr. Foley approaches her and puts his hand on her shoulder to turn her toward him in order to get her full attention. Sheila immediately backs up and mutters, "Don't touch me. Who are you anyway?"

Mr. Foley's frustration is at a high level now because he sees this hallway violation as a repeated problem that should be easily taken care of by the school's leadership team. He drops his hand, but responds in a frustrated hushed whisper voice, "I'm the testing coordinator." Sheila responds with a glib, "My teacher gave me permission so you can't tell me I can't go to the bathroom."

Mr. Foley ignores this and responds, "You know no one is supposed to be in this area. Other students are testing and you are being very disrespectful to them." Sheila immediately stands a little taller and returns the tone, commenting, "I wasn't bothering anyone. This class isn't testing. I'm going to the bathroom, and my teacher gave me permission."

As Sheila attempts to walk away, Mr. Foley interjects, "Oh, no you don't. We're going back to your classroom so that we can address this with your teacher. She needs to know that you violated this area and I need to remind her about the rules." As they walk back toward the classroom, Mr. Foley continues his negative comments, venting his frustration about the testing guidelines, which draws attention from other students who are passing by. With each step, Sheila's head hangs lower and lower as she dreads the confrontation in front of her classroom.

*(**Unintended consequence:** One of the students Mr. Foley passes on his way back to Sheila's classroom is Jacob, a second grader who has enjoyed being in the robotics club that Mr. Foley sponsors after school. Jacob is surprised to see Mr. Foley "being mean" to another student and is even a little scared of the look on Mr. Foley's face. Later that day at lunch, he tells his best friend Todd, who is also in the club, and they decide to not go to robotics this week to give Mr. Foley time to cool off.)*

Alternative Approach to Vignette V: The Testing Coordinator

There are many issues at play here, from the obvious—Mr. Foley's frustration with the testing guidelines that has very little to do with Sheila—to the realistic issue that Sheila uses Mr. Foley's position as a part-time person at the school as an attempt to gain leverage in the power struggle. An additional layer that is not obvious in our vignette is that Mr. Foley's cultural background also lends itself to a "children respect adults, period" mentality. Let's begin with Mr. Foley's frustrations.

As a school leader, it's important to have a strong handle on issues that plague the staff who have a part-time presence in your school. It's not unusual for these staff members to most often and most quickly become frustrated with school procedures, feel left out of the decision-making process, and generally feel devalued. Your proactive understanding of this dynamic and willingness to act on this understanding will be the basis of preventing exactly this type of situation.

Ask yourself these questions: What deliberate actions do you take to get to know your part-time staff? How do you include them in the processes used by your school team to make decisions? Do you remember them when celebrating staff accomplishments? Do you take steps to ensure they are in the communication loop?

If you answered yes to many of these questions, then it is highly likely that Mr. Foley's frustration levels will not reach the point indicated in the vignette and, therefore, this type of power struggle is more likely to be avoided. It's important to both allow Mr. Foley to create and implement his testing guidelines, for example, and to support him in the implementation of them.

You can support him by giving him access to school staff to get everyone on the same page. You can support him by creating a monitoring schedule during testing times that includes administrators. Perhaps consider ideas that make you more visible during testing windows (i.e., move a desk into the testing hallway and work from there) so that you can help with potential disruptions and leave Mr. Foley to the work of coordinating testing.

In the case of the power struggle happening before you have put these suggestions into action or before you've had a chance to include Mr. Foley in the professional development on power struggles, a follow-up with him will be critical. As the scenario plays out, you likely now have one frustrated testing coordinator, one defensive classroom teacher, and one humiliated student (not to mention the two robotics students) to support in the aftermath.

In your discussion with Mr. Foley, give him a preview of the six strategies you've adopted as a school staff (chapter 8) to avoid power struggles. Provide him with the opportunity to consider the recent incident and have him select the steps he feels could have been alternatives in the situation with Sheila. If he struggles, encourage him to take a close look at strategies 4 and 5.

This recommendation is astute on your part both because these two strategies would be highly effective and because you know they will likely sit better with Mr. Foley's cultural beliefs. Mr. Foley struggles with the concept that students be given choices when, in his experience, children should be expected to do whatever the adult says simply because they are kids. You can find reassurance in knowing that Mr. Foley will gain a better understanding of this concept when he participates in the professional learning for power struggles.

Meanwhile, back to strategies 4 and 5. In both cases, Mr. Foley reminds the student of the importance of avoiding the testing area but ends the conversation there before it escalates. Depending on the level of perceived disrespect that he feels the student shows, he can always come back later to her classroom and talk with the teacher calmly about his concern and ask for her support in preventing this type of situation in the future.

He can also talk with Sheila directly now that they've both cooled off and work to gain her support in helping with the effort of maintain an appropriate testing environment. As a fourth grader who has been in the school several years, it is quite possible that she might offer solutions from a student perspective that haven't occurred to Mr. Foley.

Finally, as the school leader, you can acknowledge for Mr. Foley that strategy 6 is definitely a great follow-up option. This will allow you and the leadership team to work with Mr. Foley to address the recurring issue of how to maintain an appropriate testing environment, which, in turn, will empower Mr. Foley to feel more a part of the team.

Vignette VI: The Substitute

It's November and Miss Howard is substituting for the first time at the local middle school. Miss Howard has been subbing at various elementary schools since the start of the school year, but the middle level is new to her. As she checks in with the designated administrative assistant, Miss Howard admits to being a little intimidated by how big the kids are and how much more mature they seem to be. She is given a folder with her teaching schedule (that includes six different groups of students) and the advice from the secretary to "be firm so that they know who's in charge." Armed with these words of wisdom, Miss Howard proceeds to her first block class.

It's Friday morning and this group of seventh graders is definitely unruly. Miss Howard can see from the get-go that they will not easily be persuaded to get into the learning mode. As the bell rings, she surveys the group, many of whom are still meandering to their seats, talking with their friends, and generally ignoring that class is starting.

Remembering the secretary's words, Miss Howard immediately raises her voice and greets the class with: "That was the bell, girls and boys. I fail to see why you're not all already seated." This gets a general compliance by most of the group who, though startled, quickly get to their desks and start to quiet down. There are three boys in the back, however, who make a point of slowly going to their desks while throwing out comments like "Geesh, you don't have to yell," and "Who made her boss?"

Miss Howard proceeds to introduce herself and review the teacher's plan for them for the block. As she talks, one of the boys from our group, Nathan, loudly makes a snide comment to his neighbor, "Miss Howard needs to chill. It's Friday." Miss Howard walks directly to his desk and demands that he repeat himself. She is convinced at this point that she will need to make an example of this one if she's to keep the class in line. Nathan slides down in his seat a bit and mumbles "Nothing."

Unfortunately, Miss Howard presses the point. "No, really, if you have something to say, speak up." Nathan stays silent and begins to get red in the face as a result of Miss Howard's prodding. Once more, Miss Howard insists, "Young man, you can repeat yourself here or go into the hall for the block." At that, Nathan stands up, shoves his books off his desk, and leaves the classroom. Seeing this reaction as a "win," Miss Howard looks at the rest of the class and states, "I may be a substitute but hopefully now you all know I mean business."

*(**Unintended consequence:** Back in the main office when Miss Howard was picking up her substitute packet, Mr. Jett, another regular substitute was doing the same. At hearing the secretary advise Miss Howard to be firm and show them who's boss, Mr. Jett began to worry that perhaps it was the secretary's way of sending him an indirect message. Mr. Jett was generally*

liked by the students and always tried to be upbeat and flexible with them. He was an effective substitute but walked out of the office questioning whether he needed to have a firmer hand with the kids to ensure that the other adults didn't see him as a pushover.)

Alternative Approach to Vignette VI: The Substitute

At the core of this vignette is the powerful message that as the school leader, you must have a plan of action on how to prepare your substitutes to address power struggles with the students, maintaining the same expectations as your full-time staff. It's an unfortunate fact that substitutes fill classrooms in our school every day and, thus, have a profound effect on student learning. To leave them to their own devices is a huge mistake that can cost students dearly when it comes to time spent on teaching and learning.

To that end, your first step is to reflect on how you choose substitutes for your building. Are you cultivating relationships with substitutes in order to ensure that you have a core group of effective substitutes from which to pick each day? Once you know the folks who will be subbing in your building, how do you convey to them the critical information they need to know to be with your team for a day, a week, a month, or even for a whole school year in some instances?

Undoubtedly, many of you are responding to these questions with a general sense that you have no control over the substitutes hired by your district. That's often true. That said, don't discount your ability to be constantly recruiting qualified folks to join the substitute pool and to choose your school as a primary location. Next up then is how you ensure they are armed with the appropriate tools to be successful each day.

Please ensure that the folks directly in charge of substitutes (whether a member of your leadership team or a secretary) understand that they are expected to convey school-wide expectations. If the secretary who met Miss Howard in the morning had been trained in your power struggles lesson and/ or knew exactly how you've agreed as a school team to engage with students presenting concerns, then she would not have given Miss Howard the "be firm" speech in the first place. Keep in mind, then, that the unintended consequence of Mr. Jett overhearing and changing his already effective approach to better meet the expectation outlined by the secretary would not happen.

Likewise, the staff overseeing subs should be prepared to be in tune with substitutes who seem nervous or anxious about their assignments. When identified, these folks can be expressly targeted for extra support. This support can take many forms: be included in professional development, be assigned a teacher mentor who can kick off their first class with them to model strategies for student interactions, be provided a link to a YouTube video that your staff creates for this exact purpose—to introduce substitutes to your school and your expectations, something they can view online before being assigned to your school. You likely have other support mechanisms in place as well, but these are a few to get you started.

In addition to these proactive measures, let's address the aftermath of Miss Howard's experience and how to address it with her. First let's acknowledge that this type of thing can happen with substitutes who already feel unempowered on a regular basis. More often than not, you may not even be aware that this has occurred. To ensure that you are aware so that you can support the substitute and the student, you'll want to have mechanisms in place that empower subs to report when situations like this arise.

Additionally, take steps to ensure that your teachers are reporting to the leadership team when a sub writes about these types of situations in their notes to the teacher (oftentimes the teacher will address the student/class, so it's important, for future reference, that you send the message to teachers that you want to have the chance to address the substitute). Likewise, encourage key staff to check in on students who are sent to the hall. Whenever you see a student sitting/standing outside a classroom, it is always prudent to ask them why they are there and provide support as necessary.

Now that you are aware of the situation, it's important to work with Miss Howard and help her see the negative ramifications of the power struggle and to help her understand more appropriate responses in the future. She will likely benefit from some general guidance on the development stages of middle schoolers and how best to understand them. The key here is to help eliminate Miss Howard's anxiety over working with students this age.

When she's ready, guide her to our six strategies. There are no wrong answers here, so encourage her to share which of the strategies she would feel comfortable using. Be sure to have her play the scenario out again to include her selected strategy(ies) so that she can clearly articulate how the situation would be resolved with this new approach. This teachable moment then becomes an opportunity to expand the conversation and provide any additional support that you identify is needed.

WRAP-UP

One major benefit of your school setting is the vast majority of adults who have come together with the unifying purpose of supporting students in this learning environment. One major challenge of your school setting is the vast majority of adults who have come together with the unifying purpose of supporting students in this learning environment. No, this is not an erroneous cut and paste.

This is a simple fact. By virtue of their individuality, the adults in your school bring with them their own unique experiences, levels of preparation to work in a school and with children, perceptions of how a school should function, and, well, baggage in general. This simple fact, then, gives way to the need to ensure that each adult, regardless of role, be well versed on both your expectations regarding student interactions and the professional learning there regarding power struggles. The time spent proactively will pay huge dividends over time.

Chapter Five

Parents and School Staff

Power Struggles That Foster the Us vs. Them Culture

Our focus thus far has been on the school staff-student relationship and how power struggles allowed to go unfettered can drastically impact student learning. This makes sense since it is the relationship that has the greatest impact on student achievement; teacher to student, school leader to student, school leader to teacher.

The culture of a school, however, is impacted regularly by yet another group of stakeholders—the parents. The impact of parents on our students' school experience is evident every day in our schools. Whether your school is known for its "helicopter" parents or is characterized by parents who rarely make an appearance, one way or another every parent impacts your school's culture.

Take, for example, the parent who works sixty hours a week and is rarely heard from by your school team. This parent impacts your school's culture based on the "message" she conveys to her child about the school. If the parent feels that the school is doing a good job, then she says as much at home, defends school staff when her child is upset by ensuring that both sides of the story are heard, and generally makes it clear to her child that he is fortunate to be attending your school and should act accordingly.

If that same parent, however, is unsatisfied with the school, then she may send a very negative message about the school to her child. The lack of satisfaction could be due to experiences or could be based solely on her sense of disconnection based on her professional commitments. In this instance, the parent makes a point to talk about school staff negatively with her child (or, perhaps, to other parents, not realizing that her child is privy to the conversations). This parent asserts that her child is always right and that any issue with school is the fault of school staff.

In both instances, you may never hear from the parent directly. In fact, this is also likely a parent whom school staff will repeatedly try to reach but can never get on the phone or via e-mail. She is rarely available for school events and sees her role as parent as home based only, not seeing the value of being involved in her child's school despite your staff's best efforts to get her involved. Make no mistake; parental distance in either case is likely to have negative effects on your culture.

On the opposite end of the spectrum is the "helicopter" parent. This parent is generally characterized by his constant presence in every facet of his child's education. This parent e-mails teachers constantly, either requesting or demanding detailed information about assignments, grading, school events, his child's behavior, or any other component of day-to-day school life. This parent never feels that he is given enough time by school staff.

Likewise, the "helicopter" parent monitors his child's every step at school. He is likely planning his child's school calendar to include organizing due dates for projects, tests, homework assignments, and so on. This parent is also the first to check on the child's grades, even before the child does, and is already questioning the teacher about less than stellar grades before the student has a chance to explain them or to ask the teacher herself.

At the younger levels, this parent may also be highly visible in the school. He volunteers to be the room dad, attends all school functions, can be a great resource for the parent-teacher organization, and so on. Keep in mind, of course, that this can be good and bad. Some parents put in countless hours with the simple intent of supporting the school's academic program for all students. Other parents might put in the same hours but for a very different purpose. These parents, sadly, are the first to share confidential information on the sidelines of the soccer fields with anyone who will listen. They like to be seen as a fountain of information and freely share their opinion—negative or positive, accurate or inaccurate.

Still a third example of parent representatives is the parent who is culturally challenged by your school. He and his family have immigrated to the United States and find schooling here drastically different from their home country. In some cases this parent hesitates to get involved with the school because he is intimidated by the unknown and is disenfranchised by the lack of communication in his native language.

This parent, too, may contribute positively or negatively. He may simply be so relieved that his child can access an education with relative safety and for free that he insists at every opportunity that the school is good. Also as likely is that, due to a language barrier, he feels ostracized and overlooked by the school and, as a result, has established a lack of trust of the school among his family.

These three examples include extremes often found in any school community. Your parent base is made up of all kinds of folks with varying degrees of involvement. Together they comprise a significant portion of your school community and, therefore, have the potential to have a large impact on its culture. As a result, it's critical that you and your school team have an agreed upon set of expectations regarding parent interactions. At the heart of these expectations continues to be the commitment to relationships that are founded on respect and that ensure that each individual's dignity is maintained no matter what.

IT STARTS WITH YOU: THE LEARNING

You're likely wondering, now, what these protocols or expectations should include? Your collective expectations regarding parent interactions will be a proactive mechanism used by all of your staff to ensure that parents maintain a positive role in the scope of your school culture. The process you use to create these expectations will be the same collaborative process you use when establishing any school-wide expectations. You'll want to provide the opportunity for all staff members to be at least represented in the discussion so that you ensure a comprehensive set of expectations that cross all domains. Though ultimately you are better served creating your own with your team, we've outlined some starting points here.

Establish Basic Communication Expectations

How often are staff members expected to have proactive communication with parents? As the school leader you will model proactive communication with your electronic newsletter, regularly scheduled e-mail/phone blasts, and so on. These are your ways of showing how effective it can be to keep parents in the know. The commitment to this simple concept pays huge dividends in parents feeling like they know what's happening and that you value their input.

The same holds true for your staff members. Depending on their roles, it is appropriate to establish an expected frequency with which they should communicate. You see some teachers do this independently by sending home weekly notes or e-mails that outline what's going on in class, upcoming major deadlines, how parents can be helpful, and so forth. At the other end of the spectrum are teachers who never communicate and only respond when a parent reaches out to them. Don't leave this standard up to the teacher; instead, as a team, agree on the standard (this also goes a long way, by the way, in preventing pitting teachers against one another). A good compromise is that the teacher sends something out at least monthly.

Along these same lines, include an expectation about the communication of grade information. Is a teacher expected to reach out to a parent when a student's grade reaches a certain level (I trust your answer is *yes*)? What is the time frame? Many schools now have electronic systems whereby parents can set up the system to e-mail them when grades hit certain marks.

A best practice is that teachers are not permitted to allow the system to replace their more personalized communication. It's still important that the teacher acknowledges that she's paying attention to the grade by sending a quick e-mail on her own encouraging the parent to check in with the student at home and sharing some pointers on what the student can do to improve. Again, this proactive communication goes a long way toward minimizing the reactionary e-mails a teacher fields when grades are published.

Establish Some Basic Parent Communication Reminders

What should staff be keeping in mind when communicating with parents? No one—kids or adults, parents or staff—likes to enter into communication with someone, knowing that there is an established hierarchy that they cannot overcome. Yes, the staff member is an education expert, but treating that position as a position of power when dealing with a parent will only encourage a power struggle.

Instead, it's important to be open-minded. Yes, for example, teachers have established protocols, and they want to be consistent. They also, however, have to acknowledge that if the parent did not have any voice in the creation of those protocols, then it is perfectly natural for him to question them. Questioning protocols is not always an act of disrespect; more often than not it is an effort to seek to understand. If staff members approach parental questions with this in mind, even with those parents who are confrontational, they'll find that they are less likely to end up in a power struggle.

In the case where the parent is contacting you because his child reported something that has caused him some concern, remember that first and foremost, he only has his child's perspective in the beginning. Hopefully, the parent will acknowledge this himself: "My son shared something and I realize it's only his perspective which is why I'm calling you to get yours," for example. If not, then it's important for the staff member to establish this up front, "Thanks so much for reaching out to me. I certainly understand that you have your son's perspective, and I appreciate that you understand that there are always two perspectives and it's important to get both to understand the situation," and then move into the next phase of the conversation.

As the school leader, you understand that there are two sides to every story and oftentimes the truth lies somewhere in the middle. This is true when the situation involves kids, adults, anyone. What's important about this part of your protocol is that you help all of your staff understand that no one version of a story retold is usually 100 percent accurate—not because anyone is intentionally being dishonest but simply because our memories are not usually designed to pick up on every nuance, and whichever nuances we do latch onto will be different depending on our role. In other words, though the staff member may recall accurately what she said to the student, she may not know that her facial expression was sending a different message, one that the student picked up on and now has as part of his recollection.

Establish a Set Response Time

How quickly will staff be expected to respond to a parent communication? Twenty-four hours? Forty-eight hours? Once established, make it clear to the team that there can be no exceptions to this, otherwise you'll be amazed at the number of excuses folks can come up with to delay a response to even the simplest of parent requests or communication. This is not to discount that teachers are some of the busiest professionals out there.

Instead, it's important to note that the expectation is there for a reason and, when followed, usually results in less of a time commitment in the long run. It takes a lot longer to defuse an irate parent who feels he was ignored than to address a concern in a timely manner.

Establish a Method of Documenting

How will staff document that their communications with parents meet school and district expectations? Though this really only becomes important when a review of the record is necessary, practicing each time with the set method ensures that there are no issues in creating a documentation trail when necessary.

Establish a Meeting Protocol

When a parent requests to meet with a staff member, what is the appropriate environment, time, and so on? This can be a tricky question, as some staff will demonstrate a lack of comfort about meeting with a parent privately. You may establish that one-on-one meetings are fine but that staff can call upon a counselor or administrator to attend if necessary. Likewise, establish that the classroom is an appropriate setting unless the staff member prefers a more public setting like office space in the main office, a quiet corner in the library, or another setting.

What if there is tension with the parent over a disagreement? How does the protocol change? Staff could be encouraged to request a department chair, counselor, or administrator be involved if the situation is already tense. This both offers support to the staff member and shows the parent that your team is committed to finding resolution. If a joint meeting is to occur, make sure the folks involved know to discuss in advance who will lead the discussion, what the intended outcomes are, and how decisions will be made.

Establish a Protocol for Conversations with Parents (Whether in Person or over the Phone)

What are some key strategies that staff can use in conversations with parents that are more likely to lead to successful outcomes? This is an opportunity to role-play discussions with parents. Encourage staff to start conversations by establishing the purpose of the conversation (you asked me to call/meet to discuss _____) and asking the parent to share his concern and to listen attentively without interrupting. It's important that the parent feel heard.

This is tough to do, especially when the parent is misinformed. That said, listening first goes a long way toward establishing a sense of collaboration. Before responding, share that you value the parent's input and acknowledge that he knows his child best. You may or may not agree that the parent does know his child best. That said, there's no discounting the years he has spent raising the child, so don't try to; it will get you nowhere. Next go ahead and offer your response, keeping in mind strategy 2 from chapter 8.

Use positive language and a calm tone. Once you've shared your response, establish next steps. Are your perspectives similar enough that you can reach a mutually agreed-upon resolution? If so, then proceed and be sure to end the conversation by restating the agreed-upon next steps. If you determine that resolution is not likely between the two of you, suggest a second conversation with a department chair or administrator present. You are looking for someone who can facilitate the conversation and, with an outsider's perspective, help you to come to consensus.

Establish a Follow-Up Procedure

Now that the communication is complete, how does the staff member follow up? Follow-up is a crucial piece. Whether follow-up is necessary can be established when finalizing next steps. It's important for the parent to know that the agreed-upon steps are happening. It's a great idea to agree on a follow-up phone call or e-mail and agree on a time frame, "I'll e-mail you at the end of next week to share how it's going in the classroom and to hear from you how the conversation went with your child at home." Though staff members may disagree, the onus of follow-up is usually on them, and being proactive with follow-up is the best way to guarantee that the issue does not come up again in the future.

One final thought on these protocols: Be sure your staff knows that your collaborative agreement on how to treat others and maintain their dignity certainly also includes themselves. No staff member should feel that she has to be a verbal punching bag for someone else, regardless of the person's role.

If she feels she is being treated unfairly or that her dignity is being disregarded, then it is appropriate to simply state, "I'm not okay with being spoken to this way so I'm going to end our conversation for now. I will get back to you once I've spoken with an administrator on how to proceed. It's important to me that we resolve this situation, but we cannot do that if one or both of us is treating the other this way."

THE PRACTICE

This next series of vignettes will spotlight just a few examples of the types of power struggles that can be created when you have not established expectations among your school team. The examples will make clear the need for professional development for your team in order to ensure that they have the opportunity to brainstorm potential parent issues and to even role-play how to address issues when they occur.

Vignette I: The Dominator

Mrs. Walker is the mother of a fourth grader, Darren, who has a significant physical disability. Darren has been at the school since kindergarten and the staff has worked closely with Mrs. Walker since the beginning to provide a free appropriate public education for Darren. The nature of Darren's disability is such that he is prone to injury. His fragility has undoubtedly led to his mom being hyper-involved in every aspect of his school day. Over the years, Mrs. Walker has become increasingly demanding of staff and will often resort to bullying tactics to get her way. Mrs. Walker is well known by district- and state-level special education staff due to her propensity to take legal action when she doesn't get what she wants.

This school year started with Mrs. Walker working with a new case manager for Darren. At his first IEP meeting Mrs. Walker expressed her displeasure at having a new teacher assigned and demanded to choose the case manager. Mr. Beck, the special education teacher, politely stood his ground and verified his qualifications to be assigned to Darren. The assistant principal maintained her commitment to Mr. Beck's assignment.

That evening, Mrs. Walker sent an inflammatory e-mail to the teacher and sent copies to the assistant principal, principal, and district special education director. In it she accused the school staff of working against her and not considering Darren's safety needs. Specifically, she attacked the teacher as inexperienced and the assistant principal as insensitive. Mrs. Walker demanded that the case manager be changed immediately.

Mrs. Walker has a habit of including her entire history with the school in every e-mail. She will often take tangents that result in pages and pages of information that have nothing to do with the current concern but everything to do with intimidating the reader. Mr. Beck read the e-mail, his first from her, at home that evening and was offended and became defensive. He responded immediately, replying to all, insisting that he was more than qualified to be case manager and questioning Mrs. Walker's ability to make that determination. His response appeared to be an attempt to establish a power position.

Mrs. Walker replied in kind and, in an effort to demonstrate a position of power, demanded another meeting immediately to include the district director of special education. Mr. Beck replied, insisting that no further meeting was necessary and stating his reluctance to participate in a conversation about something that had already been discussed and decided.

At this point, the principal interjected and suggested that all parties meet again, this time with her present, to address the concerns. As a result of her long history with Mrs. Walker, the principal knew just how volatile Mrs. Walker could become and she realized it was best to mitigate the situation and the growing power struggle personally.

*(**Unintended consequence:** As a new teacher, Mr. Beck is unaware that Mrs. Walker is deeply entrenched in the parent group at the school. Though she is amenable to working with the principal to resolve the situation, she contacts several parents prior to the meeting and bashes Mr. Beck's performance. Down the road, this will take its toll in that Mr. Beck will have to work harder to establish trust with parents).*

Alternative Approach to Vignette I: The Dominator

This vignette is a great example of how complex power struggles can become as well as how important it is that your school team establishes early on protocols for dealing with difficult parents. Had Mr. Beck been better prepared with the protocols we discussed earlier, he would have known not to respond immediately to Mrs. Walker's e-mail but, instead, to give both her and himself a chance to cool off (while still meeting a twenty-four- or forty-eight-hour response window).

Responding right away almost always ensures that a power struggle will ensue, simply because e-mail lends itself to becoming volatile more quickly than the same interaction in person. Electronic communication means not having to see the recipient's response, note their defensive body language, and so on. The lack of insight that comes from having these visual cues can set the stage for greater levels of volatility.

As a result of the back-and-forth e-mails that ensue, both Mr. Beck and Mrs. Walker become more defensive and more confrontational. It now becomes incumbent on you as the school leader to facilitate the situation. Set up a time to meet with Mrs. Walker later the next day, to allow you time to meet with Mr. Beck beforehand, both to discuss how to better handle this type of situation in the future and to brainstorm how to reach a resolution in the meeting with the parent in a way that ensures that both parent and teacher maintain their dignity. Your goal is that both walk away feeling a balance of power.

In your conversation with Mr. Beck, you first reflect back on the learning from chapter 8. Does he see when the power struggle began? Can he identify at what point his own actions contributed to the power struggle rather than working to prevent the power struggle? In the event that Mr. Beck cannot identify these points, then you will walk him through them.

Mostly, you want him to see that it is never a good idea, whether in person or electronically, to respond to a parent when you sense that you are on the defensive. This can only lead to negative interactions. There is no question that strategy 4, delay the interaction, would have served him well with respect to Mrs. Walker's e-mail.

Mr. Beck should understand that, in the do-over, he would wait to respond to the e-mail until the next morning (plenty of time to still meet the agreed-upon twenty-four- or forty-eight-hour response time you've agreed on) and, even better, until after he's had a chance to talk with the assistant principal, who understands better how to work with Mrs. Walker. In doing so, the assistant principal can then share that it's always best to give Mrs. Walker a little time because she will often retract her original confrontational communication when given time to cool off.

The assistant principal can also share that it is her responsibility to explain how case managers are assigned and to get Mrs. Walker to the point of acceptance. It's also important that Mr. Beck understand he is not in a position to have to defend himself. The fact that he was assigned to Darren is evidence enough that the school team believes he is qualified to fulfill the role.

Now it's time to brainstorm about the meeting later that day. Your intention, of course, is to help Mrs. Walker accept the new case manager assignment. You'll explain to Mr. Beck that, given the nature of the e-mail exchange, you will start the meeting by apologizing to both the teacher and parent that the conversation became negative and acknowledge that you understand why both of them felt, and therefore responded, the way they did.

You'll reiterate your suggestion to Mr. Beck that any e-mails he receives like this one in the future are to be held onto until he has had a chance to get administrator support on how to respond. This is stated in front of the parent so that she understands your support for her getting a response while also understanding that you support the teacher and don't expect him to simply give in to her bullying tactics.

The meeting will proceed with your working to gain a better understanding of the parent's concerns and then addressing those concerns as appropriate. The outcome of the meeting will be driven entirely by how the conversation goes. Making a change like this, simply because a demand is made by a parent, is not usually a good idea. You go down a rocky road headed toward the squeaky-wheel-gets-the-oil syndrome when you react in that manner. Be cautious. Instead, it is much more effective for the long term to show the parent how her concerns can be alleviated, by sharing information you may have about the case manager and the situation that the parent did not previously know. That said, it's important to weigh decisions based on the information presented, so that's how you will proceed.

Let's wrap up this vignette by addressing the unintended consequence mentioned earlier. You may not know right then that Mrs. Walker has been spreading negativity about Mr. Beck (although given your history with her, this is likely a pattern) but you're astute enough to predict the possible consequences of the interaction.

To that end, it's a good idea to include in your wrap-up of the meeting a statement that acknowledges how much you appreciate both the teacher and the parent keeping this conversation confidential: "I know you both understand how important it is to Darren and all of us that these types of conversations are kept confidential. It doesn't help anyone if we are talking to other teachers or parents about the disagreement, especially as we strive to work together positively in the future. Thank you for maintaining one another's confidentiality."

Vignette II: The Warpath

Mrs. Jonas is a middle school parent who is very involved with the school. She is active in the PTA and is generally supportive of the school community as a whole. This particular Wednesday Mrs. Jonas arrived in the main office and asked for a visitor's pass to her daughter's science classroom. Mrs. Jenkins, the front office receptionist, thought this was unusual because this was the very period that Jessica had science, which meant that the teacher was currently teaching.

"I'm sorry, Mrs. Jonas. Jessica's science teacher has a class this period." "I know," Mrs. Jonas interrupted, "Jessica just texted me from there. I'm not happy at all with the teacher and I'm going to see her now." Mrs. Jenkins immediately responded, "You can't do that, Mrs. Jonas. You'll have to e-mail or call her to set up a meeting." Mrs. Jonas interrupted her, "You don't understand, I know she won't admit what she's done if I wait, so I want the chance to talk to her right now." "I can't let you go to her classroom, Mrs. Jonas," Mrs. Jenkins responded with a stronger tone to her voice.

"Interrupting her entire class is not an option." "Fine, then let me see the principal. I'm going to talk to someone right now."

*(**Unintended consequence:** Stephanie, another sixth grader, is waiting in the front office to see the nurse. She has the same science teacher in another period and immediately begins to make assumptions about what the teacher could have done. She quickly tweets on her phone, "Aww, Mrs. Snyder's in trouble." And so the re-tweeting began. By lunchtime, the science teacher has heard about the tweet from another student and is on the principal's doorstep demanding action.)*

Alternative Approach to Vignette II: The Warpath

As your front office receptionist, Mrs. Jenkins is generally supportive of and helpful to parents. They see her as a positive resource. It surprised her to see Mrs. Jonas in this state, and she was unprepared to handle the situation. The simple opportunity to participate in professional development, like that described earlier in this chapter, will go a long way toward helping someone like Mrs. Jenkins avoid this type of situation. Once Mrs. Jonas showed any signs of agitation, Mrs. Jenkins was out of her element, as evidenced by the fact that she simply kept reacting to the parent instead of quickly summing up the situation and suggesting an alternative to letting the scene play out in the front office.

As you work with her afterward, you will remind her of the strategies from chapter 8. You'll likely agree that strategies 1, offer choices, and 2, maintain positive words and tone, were key intervention options. Once Mrs. Jonas refused to give up on the idea of going to the classroom, Mrs. Jenkins moved into negative mode by using words like "can't" and "that isn't an option." These types of words serve to shut down the recipient with respect to them hearing you. At this point, the recipient usually shifts fully into "proving you wrong" mode.

In the future, Mrs. Jenkins will understand that any time an interaction is turning negative, it's important to move it to a more private setting. The front office is always full of members of your school community and should be the last place a power struggle is permitted to occur. Once in the more private setting, Mrs. Jenkins can then consider choices that can be offered to Mrs. Jonas. "I understand that you are upset. Would you like to explain to me what your daughter texted about or would you like to talk with an administrator so that he can support you?"

This simple act shows that Mrs. Jenkins acknowledges that Mrs. Jonas is legitimately concerned (versus simply denying her request by not showing any concern at all over what her daughter may be experiencing). Though the receptionist is correct in not allowing the parent to proceed to the classroom at that point, she never bothered to ask what exactly the problem was. What if the daughter texted that she had just been hit by the teacher? An extreme example, yes, but one that makes the point that you're going to want to know what the concern is that brought a parent to the school right away. This small step alone ensures that you are always making safety a priority.

Once the receptionist better understands the nature of the concern, she is better equipped to decide how to proceed. It is clear that the parent will need to talk with someone, so have a protocol prepared for that instance. Who among your team is the "go-to" for walk-in parents who are upset or agitated? That person then picks up where the receptionist leaves off and works to determine the next appropriate steps.

Keep in mind, of course, our tweeter. Once the confrontation was moved to a private area, the tweeter had nothing to tweet about. At most, she may have commented that Mrs. Jonas (whom she knows because she is friends with her daughter) just showed up mad. Yes, we'd prefer that even that didn't get tweeted, but that is the world in which we live. As an aside, however, it's a great piece to include in your training with staff and even to share in your conversations with parents. We cannot remind folks enough that any public areas of the school are just that, public. Anything you say or do can and will likely end up on the Internet.

The next two vignettes will be presented a bit differently. Rather than walk you through the vignette and alternative approach separately, we will share these out in their original form. You'll see that the situations are resolved successfully and no alternative approach is needed. We share them here as a model, if you will, to be used.

Both are very real examples of how misinterpreted power struggles can occur due to the array of cultural barriers we face each day in our schools. Again, these are exactly the type of scenarios you'll want to present to staff, both in discussing power struggles and in addressing your agreed-upon practices when it comes to parents.

Vignette III: The Cultural Barrier

"We need an administrator in the cafeteria." Like most school leaders, Mr. Simpson never liked hearing those words. It was early, and school had not even started yet. As was true with most days at this high school, however, students often congregated in the cafeteria to eat breakfast and socialize while they waited for the day to begin. As Mr. Simpson hurried to the cafeteria, he had thoughts of food fights, student altercations, pranks . . . all sorts of possibilities.

When he arrived, he was surprised that the disruption occurring actually centered on a parent and a student. The parent, Mr. Cuevas, was talking loudly in Spanish to his son, Joseph, who in turn was sinking lower and lower into his seat at the table. Mr. Cuevas grabbed his son by the arm, indicating that he wanted him to get up and come with him. Other students had backed away in alarm, very much unsure of what to do. Mr. Simpson approached and in a calm voice offered his support.

"Good morning. Can I help you gentlemen with something today?" Obviously very agitated, Mr. Cuevas launched into a string of Spanish in a tone that was confrontational and harsh. Mr. Simpson, seeing the alarm of the other students, responded, "Why don't we go to my office and we can discuss the problem." There was clearly a language barrier and Mr. Cuevas grabbed his son again, attempting to drag him from the cafeteria.

At this point, Mr. Simpson was sure he didn't think it was a good idea for them to leave with the father in this state. He asked the young man to interpret what his father was now yelling, and Joseph responded by beginning to yell himself at his father. At that point, Mr. Simpson became frustrated and raised his own voice "That's enough. Tell your dad we're going to my office."

Joseph proceeded to ignore him. Mr. Simpson saw his lead custodian nearby and gestured for him to come over. "Mr. Shan, can you please ask this gentleman if he will come to my office with me?" Mr. Shan did so and immediately Mr. Cuevas began to calm down and shake his head yes. It was clear that he wanted the chance to speak with Mr. Simpson.

After arriving in his office, Mr. Simpson called for a parent liaison who could interpret the conversation. When she arrived and introduced everyone, Mr. Simpson asked that she ask Mr. Cuevas to share his concerns so that they could work together toward resolution. As it turns out, Mr. Cuevas was there in the cafeteria that morning because his son, a tenth grader, had not come home the night before.

Mr. Cuevas reminded Mr. Simpson that his family had only been in the United Stated for one year. In the beginning, Joseph was every bit the good son he had always been. In the last few months, however, Joseph had become combative. He refused to follow his parents' rules, insisted that things were different for American high schoolers—they don't have curfews, their parents don't tell them what to do, and so on.

At this point, Mr. Cuevas looked at Mr. Simpson and made a simple request, "Will you please explain to my son in front of me how parenting goes with American parents? My son seems to think his mother and I are not very smart." Mr. Simpson chuckled and happily proceeded to facilitate the conversation between father and son about reasonable expectations, and so forth.

He was careful to acknowledge for Joseph how hard it is to acclimate to a new culture, while also sending a strong message that using this as an excuse to do whatever he wanted was not okay. Needless to say, by the end of the conversation, Joseph was frustrated and a bit sheepish but understood that *he would not be continuing to pull the wool over his parents' eyes, and Mr. Cuevas left feeling supported by the school.*

Was it Mr. Simpson's "job" to have this conversation? Did it have anything to do with teaching and learning? Well, *yes* to both. If a large part of our responsibility is to create a learning environment that is conducive to teaching and learning, then addressing the whole child has to be a part of our responsibility. We can't lament about how much the home front impacts what we do (whether positively or negatively) and then also pass up the opportunity to have a positive impact on the home front. This is what our partnership with parents is all about.

Vignette IV: When the Bully Becomes the Bullied

Ms. Paulas is an experienced guidance counselor and is in her tenth year as a part of the counseling team at her urban high school. Over the years, she has built strong relationships with students, staff, and parents and is often a mentor to other counselors. On Friday, Mrs. Paulas is approached by a ninth-grade girl whom she sees frequently in her office. This particular young lady is prone to drama. In other words, she tends to gravitate toward other girls who create a cycle of drama among the group members.

Any given day, the whole group is upset with one member for something; they attack her verbally in person as well as viciously online, and then, like magic, the next day everyone is besties again. The cycle is ongoing and never ending despite the best efforts of various school staff to educate the girls about friendship, treating one another with dignity, and making the choice to stay away from one another if they can't be positive.

Not surprisingly, then, when Elly approaches Mrs. Paulas, the counselor is not particularly alarmed. She sits and listens patiently about yet another breakdown in the group, this time with Elly as the target. Just like the other girls when it was their turn, Elly is devastated and angry that they would treat her so poorly. Mrs. Paulas makes an earnest effort to help Elly see how the behavior she is experiencing now is exactly the same behavior she directed toward another friend in the group just two short weeks ago.

Elly fails to see the similarities and insists she is being bullied and wants action taken. Mrs. Paulas follows procedure and offers Elly the opportunity to complete a Student Incident Report, which will then be handed over to an administrator. Once she completes the report, Mrs. Paulas walks Elly back to class and considers her role in the situation over.

Monday morning arrives and Mrs. Paulas opens her e-mail to find not one but three e-mails from Elly's mom, Ms. Tide. The nature of all three e-mails is the same. Ms. Tide is demanding to know what will be done to punish the girls who bullied her daughter. Mrs. Paulas is particularly frustrated as she was unable to get Ms. Tide to respond to her e-mails earlier in the month when she reached out to talk about Elly's behavior toward another girl. Mrs. Paulas opts to hold off on responding until later in the morning while she reflects on how to approach the mom. This seems like a reasonable response time to her, given her understanding of the student and the situation.

About half an hour before school starts, the secretary calls in to let Mrs. Paulas know that Ms. Tide is in the main office demanding to see an administrator. Really frustrated now, Mrs. Paulas heads to the main office area to talk with Mom. Upon entering the office, Mrs. Paulas finds Ms. Tide speaking loudly to her daughter about how she will not tolerate her daughter being bullied and how she is going to handle these people. Her amplified voice is having the desired impact in that she is creating an audience in the area. As Mrs. Paulas approaches, Ms. Tide even turns to another parent in the office and states, "I hope your kid's not getting bullied because these people don't take it seriously."

At that, Mrs. Paulas greets Ms. Tide and asks that she follow her to her office to talk. Ms. Tide is having none of that. She's enjoying her audience. "No, I'm not going anywhere with you. You had your chance to fix this on Friday and you didn't. Now it just got worse over the weekend. Do you know what those girls wrote about my daughter on Twitter?" Before she can go further, Mrs. Paulas interrupts again and prompts her to come with her. She is trying to be understanding, but her voice level has slipped into a higher octave as a result of her desire to get to a private area.

Ms. Tide immediately takes issue with her tone and responds "Oh sure, you get me back there out of the way and then still don't do anything. No, I'm not going anywhere without seeing the principal." Now Elly is cringing in her seat, no doubt trying to be invisible. Her mom is usually calm and reasonable; she is surprised by how out of control things seem to be getting.

Mrs. Paulas looks at Elly and says, "See what I mean when I tell you there are unintended consequences to how you and your friends behave toward one another? Look at how upset your mom is right now." This sends Ms. Tide into a whole new realm of upset, and she begins to cry. "Don't talk to her. You don't talk to her. She's been through enough."

At this moment, the principal enters the office, and Ms. Tide's tears only increase, seemingly with relief at knowing she is going to talk to someone who will do something about her daughter being bullied. The power struggle between Mrs. Paulas and Ms. Tide immediately dissipates and she, Elly, and Ms. Tide join the principal in her office.

Given the hostile and emotional state of the mom, the principal begins by asking Elly to share her concerns and to give her details about what has occurred. Elly proceeds to describe a typical situation in her group of friends, though; because she is the target this time, it doesn't feel so good. The principal then asks Ms. Tide to share why she is here and what she wants to have happen.

This is the principal's way of ensuring that the parent feels she has a voice and that she understands exactly what outcomes the parent is hoping for right up front. Ms. Tide launches into the emotional devastation her daughter has felt this weekend due to the ongoing behavior of her friends. She describes their behavior as bullying and wants to know what the school will do about it. She believes all of the girls involved should be punished and that strong punishment will ensure they leave her daughter alone.

Next, the principal turns to Mrs. Paulas. The counselor relates what Elly reported to her on Friday. She expands on it to share the constantly changing dynamics of the friend group and even asks direct questions of Elly to demonstrate that Elly is very aware of these dynamics. She asks Elly to share with her mom some of the strategies they have talked about in the past with this group and probes Elly's own behavior at times. At one point, Mrs. Paulas asks Elly what she's most upset about, and Elly admits that her friends are excluding her because, despite the attacks, she most wants to be back "in" with the group.

It becomes clear that her mom only has one part of the bigger story. Ms. Tide absorbs this and slowly begins to acknowledge that this behavior toward her daughter is not in isolation. She even goes so far as to acknowledge that her daughter is a part of the problem. At that point, she becomes emotional again. This time, she turns to her daughter to ask how she could behave that way knowing what she does about her mom's history.

Ms. Tide shares that she was severely bullied in high school. She describes ongoing and pervasive attempts by other girls to strip her of her self-confidence and self-esteem and shares that it worked for a time. She has an inherent distrust of school staff because she tried to get help back then and was met with a "deal with it, you'll all grow out of it" attitude. To this day, she carries the scars of the experience.

Having heard about Ms. Tide's own experience, both the principal and counselor now better understood her reactions. They took the time to talk about how Elly's circumstances differed from her mom's so that her mom could better understand why Mrs. Paulas responded the way she did. What Mom mistook as a lack of urgency was really Mrs. Paulas pausing before responding, given the history among the girls.

Both women reflected on Ms. Tide's experience in high school and used it to explain how they have responded in similar situations at their school. Their intent was to ensure that Ms. Tide was well versed in how the school staff handles any acts of students stripping other students of their dignity. All of this had the intended effect in that Ms. Tide was consoled and felt heard. Most importantly, though, she left feeling confident that her daughter was being well cared for at school.

What started in the main office as an escalating power struggle between counselor (attempting to do the right thing by moving the spectacle out of the public eye) and parent (committed to making sure her daughter got the justice she never got as a teen) eventually evolved into an opportunity for school staff to show support for a student and her mom while also holding the student accountable for the circumstances. Now's your chance to reflect on how the school leader was able to bring this situation to a positive conclusion. What actions did the principal take that resulted in all parties feeling like they were walking away from the situation having gotten what they wanted?

We've talked previously about the importance of voice. More often than not, the root of any conflict, especially any power struggle, is the sense on the part of the participants that their voice is not being heard. The principal made it clear from the moment she approached Ms. Tide in the main office that her voice would be heard.

Likewise, she showed a commitment to giving everyone their voice so that each could create what would become a complete picture. The principal understood that any one missing voice would mean that the picture was skewed. She also realized that the student's voice would lead to a greater understanding without simply accusing Elly of making too much of what had occurred.

Again we see the role that school leaders play in "counseling" families. Was Ms. Tide's emotional response to her childhood experiences pertinent to the discussion about Elly? Some could argue, not really. The principal here, however, gets that all of Ms. Tide's "stuff" is wrapped up in her daughter's experience so, for that reason, yes it is absolutely pertinent. Did taking time to process mom's "stuff" take more of the principal's day, perhaps even keep her from other things? Yes. Was it important enough to, say, miss out on time in classrooms? Well, only you can answer that.

It's a delicate balance as we all know. Sometimes, you have to put parents on hold to keep instruction the main thing. That said, sometimes you have to put parents first in order to, well, put kids first. The important thing is that you understand it for the balancing act it is and be respectful of the act. Erring on any one side 100 percent of the time is the surest way to end up with damaged relationships that in turn damage culture that in turn negatively impacts student achievement.

WRAP-UP

Ultimately, our focus in chapter 5 has been on the critical impact that parents have on our school culture. Your proactive approach to how your school team will interact with and collaborate with parents will go a long way toward establishing partnerships that pay huge dividends each day. When your parents are made to feel that they are a part of the team that works daily for student success, you have succeeded in creating the "We" culture. Once again, our emphasis is on being deliberate about every facet of your school's culture. Leave nothing to chance.

Chapter Six

Staff Cliques

When Power Struggles Threaten Staff Unity

We've established that the adults in your school have by far the most pro-found effect on your culture. So what happens when the relationships be-tween adults break down? The fact is that whenever you get a large group of adults together in one space, there are always going to be issues among them. You can't make everyone like everyone. At best, however, you can insist that the adults model the agreed-upon expectation that every person treat others with respect and dignity. No exceptions.

Chapter 6 is about how to handle the situations that arise when the adults fail to adhere to this expectation. You see this manifested in many ways, and it can sometimes take the form of cliques. Whether intentional or inadvertent, cliques can form in lots of ways. Perhaps you have a grade-level team struc-ture in your school, and this structure in and of itself breeds a cliquish nature.

When folks are constantly grouped in the same way over and over, it becomes natural that they seek one another out rather than attempt to get to know others in the school. Perhaps you have a department that has a distinct group of young teachers who naturally gravitate toward one another, seem-ingly leaving the more veteran teachers on the outskirts. Perhaps you have a group of teaching assistants or paraprofessionals who feel undervalued and, as a result, tend to group up because there is safety in numbers.

IT STARTS WITH YOU: THE LEARNING

Your awareness of the tendency of humans to group this way is a key here. It is this awareness that will prompt you to create opportunities for staff to mix groups. Once again we'll emphasize the importance of being deliberate in your actions. How you do contribute to or work to minimize clique behavior? Do you always allows staff to make their own groups in meetings or professional development activities, or do you guide groups? Do you deliberately host school-wide social events to ensure the mixing of groups or leave it to departments or grade levels to host their own, thereby resulting in more division?

The fact is that this is another juncture where you'll have to make an honest assessment of your own practice. It's completely accurate that the school leader sets the tone of the school. So, what tone do you set? Do you deliberately go about connecting with staff? Are you a leader who fosters relationships, one who truly wants to understand and support the everyday work of teaching and learning?

Or, under the guise of teacher autonomy, do you foster a sense of indifference about your staff's day-to-day work? Or even worse, have you contributed to a negative environment by only paying attention when things aren't going well? If asked the question, "How often do you see your school leader in your classroom?" how would your teachers answer? Your answers to these questions, as well as your consideration of the data you collected in your survey of staff that we discussed in chapter 2, will give you a good sense of where you stand.

Let's look at just one slice of this—staff connections. One example is a school where the principal did not initiate school-wide staff events. He was content letting grade levels host their own Friday potlucks or birthday celebrations and focused on his own main office team for these types of events. So the structure set up almost looked like the main office crew had their own clique while the grade levels did their own thing.

Over time, with the exception of getting their mail, most staff didn't make their way to the main office, and many never left their grade-level houses. Did he set out to create this divided environment? We certainly didn't think so. That said, his lack of awareness certainly contributed to the division, and it was allowed to permeate the entire school.

When a new school leader took over and began to institute school-wide staff events as a way of showing gratitude for the staff it achieved two things—first, it began to create a sense of unity among the staff, and second, it created a whole new model of the school leadership team taking responsibility for regularly scheduled events to celebrate successes.

Keep in mind the power of celebrating successes. This is pertinent because often the best way to counter divisiveness among your staff is to create opportunities to celebrate their achievements together. These can be large acts like whole-school lunches or small like delivering cookies and milk to staff in their classrooms on Fridays as a way to say thanks for making it through a tough week. Over the years, I've found that school leaders are always looking for more suggestions on how to celebrate. I encourage you to host a brief discussion (it can even be electronically) among your colleagues to share ideas.

A critical form of building togetherness in your school is how you as the school leader make personal connections with your staff. How do you deliberately go about connecting with staff in a way that encourages them to speak up and be open with you? Again, there are tons of suggestions out there, and we encourage you to host a discussion. That said, we'll share a few here that have proven to be both effective and meaningful to staff.

Devote time to mapping out your "connection plan" at the start of each year. Yes, map it out. This is how you ensure that you are deliberate about it. It is your goal to ensure that every staff member (yes, this means everyone— custodians, bus drivers, teachers, the school psychologist, everyone) feels a personal connection with you. To begin, commit to the idea that every staff member receives at least three handwritten notes from you per year.

These notes have to be personal and have to be evidence to them that you are paying attention, that you "see" them. You'll be amazed at how astonished folks will be when they receive a note with a particular detail that they had no idea you are tuned in to. Now, it's a given that you can only pull this off because you are visible. You are out there. You cannot spend the majority of your day behind your desk or in the office. You have to commit to that first before you have any shot at really knowing your team.

It's effective to have your notes spread throughout the school year. Kick off the year with a note designed to pep each person up before the kids arrive. Perhaps your second note can be timed just before winter break; a sentiment to take home with them and ponder before returning.

This second note is a good time to get your whole leadership team involved if you'd like by divvying up the staff list. This gets them involved and gives you the chance to model strong leadership behavior. Just be aware that it's important that you make the criteria specific so that no one ends up with a "Great job, have a great break" note, which defeats the purpose of being personal and specific.

Your third note can come in the spring as a pick-me-up to get through the last hard push of the school year. You could vary this by making it a small note of gratitude that you can post publicly (on a classroom door, along the serving lines in the café for your cafeteria staff, etc.). It's great to see students read the notes and then express their gratitude to the staff member as well.

In addition to notes, consider making a phone call to each staff member once the school year is underway. The idea is to leave a message for each of them that simply expresses your gratitude for their efforts to get the school year started smoothly. Yes, you can send a whole-group e-mail with the same sentiment, but imagine the surprise when they check their voicemails to find a message from you. You'll find that staff members will approach you even days later to thank you and tell you stories of how their spouses heard the message and demonstrated such pride in their work. Talk about unintended consequences!

In between the notes and phone call, think about your school year month to month and consider one way per month to show gratitude or create an opportunity to connect. Two to three times per year host a "Principal Drop In." This can be a day where you park yourself in one space (choose a space big enough for several tables—maybe a career center or staff lounge), provide food all day, and invite staff to drop in throughout the day. Yes, if you feed them, they will come.

This is a time, with no formal agenda, for folks to join you, share their sentiments, and perhaps bring you up to speed on issues. You'll be pleasantly surprised at what staff will share in this informal environment and how quickly they will grow to see you as a nonthreatening entity who truly is there for support and guidance. A bonus unintended consequence is that they usually come at random times throughout the day and, therefore, visit with colleagues with whom they oftentimes have no regular contact.

Okay, so far we have timely notes, a phone call, and principal drop-ins to begin shaping our connection plan for the year. For the sake of a timeline, let's say our plan looks like this at this point:

August—Individual Note
September—Individual Phone Call
October—Principal Drop-In
December—Individual Note
February—Principal Drop-In
May—Individual Note

Six months down and five more to go for our staff connection plan. Interspersed in these anchor activities will be opportunities to combine your connection efforts with your general desire to show your gratitude for staff efforts.

One simple, inexpensive way to do this is treat carts. Choose a couple of months and arrange to have a couple of carts loaded with treats (preferably get your leadership team involved so that you can fan out around the school in the case of larger schools; again, this is a chance to model effective leadership for your team). One month perhaps do cookies and milk in the afternoon on a Friday. Another month perhaps do a breakfast cart first thing on a Monday. Still another idea is a traveling ice cream sundae cart. The idea is something quick.

Once the carts are set, you travel from classroom to classroom, workspace to workspace (don't forget the offices, kitchen, custodial break room, etc.) and serve a treat to everyone. Classrooms are great because you can apologize for interrupting instruction (it's always important to acknowledge that interrupting instruction is not done lightly) and publicly thank the staff in the room for their service and offer them a treat. Sometimes kids get involved by clapping and cheering (and, yes, they'll ask for a treat as well, which gives you a chance to single out why the staff members get the special treatment this time). It's a great pick-me-up for everyone.

That's two to three more months planned out. Now we are down to the final one or two. As you weigh your options, continue to be aware of your goal—creating opportunities to connect with staff, show your gratitude, and build the sense of togetherness. To that end, consider taking some time on a staff workday midyear to work on a team-building opportunity.

Yes, some folks will see team building as corny or goofy. That's okay. Even these folks are likely to come around and see the outcome as worth their time if you invest the time to conduct an activity that is meaningful. There are lots of great sources for team-building activities. One key, however, is to make your goal clear to the team. Be transparent about your intention to constantly promote a sense of "we."

That leaves you with just one month to plan out on your own (if you stuck to two months of treat carts). This is a time to dig deep with your team and consider what your staff would most appreciate. You'll no doubt come up with something great.

Keep in mind that this monthly framework is the concrete base for your connections and that you'll implement other initiatives to be connected on a daily and weekly basis. If you don't already, send out a weekly electronic staff newsletter that gives everyone a heads-up for the week about the schedule, special events, and so on.

Tailor it by including a weekly staff spotlight—a note from you about a particularly effective strategy you saw in action while out and about in the building the week before. And frankly, this weekly electronic communication should come from the school leader; it's not the same when it is sent out by anyone else. You may get help in putting it together, but it should be obvious to your team that you had a personal hand in it.

Another powerful connection technique is making the hallway your office. When you have those periods of time when you have to get to paperwork or e-mails, leave your office and set up shop in the hallway. Make it a different area each time, and be sure to have an extra seat for visitors.

In one school this happened by chance after a challenge with students over a coat drive one year. The principal promised that if they filled her office with coats, she'd move her office to the hallway for a day. They won. But, in the long run, so did she. In that instance, she moved it all—furniture, wall hangings, plants. The kids loved it! But what she found was that as she worked, students and staff alike, especially those who would never cross the threshold of her official office, stopped by to chat. This sparked an idea that grew each year.

Your effort will be much simpler in that you only need your laptop, a tabletop, and a couple of chairs. While in the hall, you are getting work done, providing supervision, generally being visible, and encouraging staff and students alike to spend some time with you. This strategy will have a profound effect. And consider extending beyond yourself and creating a schedule where there is always a member of your leadership team working somewhere in the hall. This becomes a proactive approach to building a sense of togetherness.

One final thought as we lead into the vignettes. Notice that all of the strategies outlined here are separate from any typical social opportunities you create for staff. It's easy to try to combine your monthly connection opportunity with, say, the annual teacher appreciation week. For our purposes, that's cheating. Be sure that your plan for connecting in the school year is in addition to your traditional gatherings. Remember, you have a specific goal, and you don't want to muddy the water by combining everything.

THE PRACTICE

Now that we've clarified the school leader's role in proactively creating a culture of togetherness as a way of minimizing adult power struggles and general conflicts that can arise among adults, let's take a look at some examples of the types of issues that can occur. Note that in these vignettes we won't go with a specific alternative as much as a general sense of how to approach a similar challenge in your school.

Vignette I: It's All in the Generation

The foreign language department has grown a lot in recent years due to the rising demand for more high-level languages. As a result, the principal, Mr. Schnider, has found that hiring has increased and the department looks very different now than it did five years ago. Mr. Schnider's hiring practice is designed to have teachers hiring teachers so there is always a member of the current team on the hiring panel.

As a result, Mr. Schnider has felt confident that the department works well together. His biggest concern is a couple of veteran teachers who have maintained an old-school approach to the classroom that is ineffective, and he is working closely with those teachers on their plans of improvement.

Today Mr. Schnider is meeting with one of these teachers to discuss a recent observation. The lesson did not go well and was dominated by teacher lecture and worksheets. His concern was reflected in his write-up for the teacher, and he anticipates a tough conversation. When the teacher, Mrs. Folan, arrives, Mr. Schnider begins by asking her for her summation of the lesson. Instead of discussing the lesson, however, Mrs. Folan launches into a tirade about her department. Nearly in tears, she reveals that the younger teachers are shunning her and several other of the more veteran teachers. She explains that the younger group has formed a clique and is purposefully excluding the veterans.

When asked to elaborate, the teacher recounted repeated exclusionary acts. She shared how the younger group now sits to the side of the workroom during lunch, behind a barrier clearly designed to dissuade the others from joining their conversation. Mrs. Folan also shared that these teacher intentionally ignore her in the hall. "I'll be walking along and pass one of them and they'll intentionally look away from me and not greet me."

Finally, she shared that the exclusion extends beyond school as well, because the younger crew will often have "collegial happy hours" that they claim are for team building and then intentionally not invite the others. She shared that she felt that all of this combined was impacting the instructional program since she was missing PLC meetings because the young teacher in charge of her PLC intentionally didn't send her the meeting invites. As a result, she found out later about the meetings and could only get notes of the discussion about curriculum rather than contribute herself.

Recently the divisiveness escalated when one of the younger teachers, Ms. Evans, lashed out at a veteran colleague, Mr. Todd, about a recent lesson she happened upon in his classroom. The two share space and there are times when one will work in the back of the room while the other is leading instruction with a class. After the class ended, Ms. Evans approached Mr. Todd and suggested that he might want to break up his lecture format into ten-minute increments in order to maintain student engagement.

Mr. Todd took great offense to her comment and reminded her that he'd been teaching for a long time, and perhaps she should be taking notes from him. Ms. Evans quickly moved into the defensive and snapped back that time in the classroom did not automatically equate to expertise, just like a lack of time didn't mean she wasn't effective. At that point, the department chair intervened and suggested they both walk away. According to Mrs. Folan, this was just one example of the power struggles that were beginning to emerge as a result of the cliquish behavior.

Mr. Schnider left the conversation feeling blindsided. How could all of this be happening in a department he had perceived as functioning well? It is clear that the cliquish behavior perceived by Mrs. Folan has to be investigated. Is she blowing things out of proportion? Is this a tactic to distract him from her ineffective poor performance? If this is happening, why hasn't the department chair brought it to his attention?

Mr. Schnider now has to formulate his next steps. Ordinarily he would coach the teacher toward taking the first steps to resolve the issue herself. In this situation, however, it is clear to him that Mrs. Folan has made some attempts already to address the cliquish behavior, with no success. Also unique here is that, not unlike with kids, adults can be intimidated by cliquish behavior in a way that makes it almost impossible for them to take action on their own.

*(**Unintended consequence:** The cliquish behavior in the foreign language department has not gone unnoticed. The department chair, a younger teacher but one who has been striving to build a bridge between the two groups, recently vented about the situation to other department chairs in a joint meeting. The math department chair shared that she has a similar issue on a smaller scale in one of her PLCs. The two agreed that Mr. Schnider needed to be brought into the loop but hesitated to tell him that their departments were struggling. This hesitation about how Mr. Schnider might react and see them as leaders spotlighted a general concern among the leadership team members regarding how stable their positions as chairs were with this principal.)*

It's easy to see how the principal in this scenario can get caught up in several different angles. First, you have the issue of an ineffective teacher and how you will go about supporting her to either improve or move on. Next you have the issue of one staff member's perception that other adults are exhibiting cliquish behavior and how to both determine the accuracy of the staff member's perception as well as quell the behavior if you ascertain that the perception is accurate. Finally, you have the issue of helping build your department chair's leadership skills so that he is better able to address the relationships among the teachers in his department in the future as well as to ensure he understands your expectations of him. So where to start?

Keep in mind that with any problem brought to your attention, your very first step is always to determine whether you personally will address it or if you will have one of your assistant principals begin the process while bringing you into the loop later (except in the case of schools where the principal is the only administrator). This reminder is offered so that you avoid the pitfall of being seen by your staff as the only problem solver on your team.

This can become impossible to manage over time and ultimately can cause more harm than good with respect to the ongoing growth of your whole team. Don't get us wrong, for some of us this is tough to do because we are problem solvers by nature. It feels great to be the "go-to person," doesn't it? Again, remind yourself, a collaborative, shared leadership approach is best.

For the sake of our example, the principal will take the lead especially since part of the process will be to build the leadership capacity of your department chair. It's best to start with your department chair in this instance. An initial conversation with him can serve three distinct purposes: you'll get his sense of the issue identified by Mrs. Folan, determine what if any steps he has already taken to resolve the issues, and demonstrate from the get-go that you have a collaborative leadership approach to problem solving.

Your conversation with the department chair reveals that Mrs. Folan's perception is correct. A contingency of his younger teachers has formed their own distinct group, separate from the more veteran teachers. You learn that he has tried to bridge the gap between the two groups (though he actually identifies more with the younger group) by modeling cooperative behavior to include continuing to sit at the large table with the core of the group for lunch, going out of his way to be polite and inclusive of everyone, and even going so far as to insisting on one day a week when the group sits together under the guise of discussing departmental business over lunch.

The most important thing that you learn from the chair is that there is a common theme among the teachers being shut out by the younger group—they are all teachers who are generally perceived as average or below average in their performance. Over the course of the school year, the chair has seen the younger, more effective, teachers' frustration evolve into an outright disdain for this group of older teachers. They view the group as ineffective and unwilling to work hard to be better.

Your school team is in its second year of implementing a PLC model. As a result of this model, teachers are talking and collaborating more than ever. A side effect of this model is that poor teaching techniques are brought to light. For many teachers, this is a good thing because the collaboration means that they have more, easier access to a variety of instructional approaches that have proven effective. They simply have to opt to try them.

In the case of this core group of teachers, it is apparent that they bring an "I don't plan to change" attitude to PLC discussions and the other teachers are fed up. For the most part, the younger teachers have kept their behavior to the "banding together" examples that Mrs. Folan provided. That said, it is escalating to the point of the two teachers openly accusing one another of providing poor lessons for kids. Your chair goes on to explain that though the level of negativity has rapidly increased in his department, he understands from other chairs that the problem is not unique to his department.

In addition to all of this, your chair shares that there are also some basic generational issues at play here. Yes, at the root of the problem is the teachers' perception of one another's performance, but he sees in the veteran teachers' actions a general sense of superiority, simply because of their age and experience. He has overheard them make comments about the characteristics of the millennials among their team and it's obvious to him that they have turned their lack of understanding of the millennial generation into one more point of contention.

Now that you have a strong sense of the issue, it's time for you and the chair to discuss a plan of action. This is where your proactive approach in the future, as described earlier in this chapter, will be key as it will ensure that these types of issues are less likely to arise. You agree that the first step is to have a courageous conversation with the entire department. The negativity has permeated most of the department so starting with individual conversations will take too long.

You want to address the concerns directly by creating a professional dialogue in which everyone feels able to speak openly. Who leads the discussion will depend on the two of you. If the department chair has the experience and skill set to do so, then have him lead so that his team sees him as the go-to person. That said, if he doesn't, then this is a good opportunity for you to model for him while setting the tone that he will take the lead as the next steps evolve.

For this whole department conversation, you'll want to set some protocols; otherwise this is the type of discussion that will get away from you. Determine at the start what the specific concern is that you are all here to address. In this case, the primary concern is that the department has become fractured and, therefore, student learning is being impacted. Some might disagree but your point is that broken relationships among teachers absolutely negatively impacts the classroom, whether directly or indirectly. Next, be clear about your expectations. One of this book's repeated expectations is that everyone treats one another with respect and in a way that ensures everyone maintains their dignity. This is a nonnegotiable.

Thus, your primary purpose today is to determine together how to overcome our differences so that we can meet this very basic expectation. You'll want to provide specific examples of how members of this team have not met this expectation (private lunches, ignoring one another, speaking disparagingly about one another—both veteran and younger teachers, etc.). Go ahead up front and acknowledge that these are perceptions, and that some may disagree with the perceptions. That disagreement does not negate the fact that if this is a perception by some, then it is worth addressing whether the behavior is intended to be hurtful or not.

Once the primary concern and purpose is outlined, it's time to open the discussion up to the group for input on (a) what they perceive as the causes of these behaviors, and (b) what they see as potential solutions to moving the team in a direction that will get them back to meeting the nonnegotiable of treating one another with respect and dignity. This is where your next protocol comes into play. First, make it clear that this isn't a venting session, nor is it a time to lash out at one another. We've identified the problem(s); we don't need to rehash that part. It's important that you not allow a small group of people to dominate the discussion (which tends to happen, especially when the topic is uncomfortable or contentious).

Consider establishing the expectation that everyone have three minutes to answer your specific prompt. For example, the first prompt is: "What do I need from my colleagues in order to move forward in a more positive manner?" Remind folks that when it is their turn, they are to answer this prompt and refrain from the temptation to respond to someone who spoke previously. As you lead the conversation, your department chair will be listing the needs identified so that you can come back to them and get clarification as you see necessary.

Be ready for the staff member who says, "I don't have any concerns or see any problems." That person still has three minutes; otherwise staff will use this approach as a strategy to get out of being completely honest and, therefore, uncomfortable. Still others will use it because they don't want to upset anyone. Encourage her to try to come up with an example and remind her that it's important for everyone to be forthcoming. As a last resort, ask her a direct question about the problem(s), based on what you already know, as a way to get her talking.

If everyone is being completely honest, then you are going to get some challenging things here. This is where folks will express their concern over the spectrum of teaching effectiveness. Some of them may express frustration that they don't see their colleagues working as hard as they do in PLC meetings (i.e., Mr. Kinder never contributes to the discussion or shares an instructional strategy). Still others will point out that they are concerned about how loosely structured some teachers' classes are, and the kids have too much freedom. Issues around the general notion of a PLC will arise. It's important that you and your department chair brainstorm all of the issues you expect to see raised here and to be prepared to address them. As always, also be prepared for surprises.

Your second prompt could be: "Based on what I've heard from my colleagues thus far, what is one thing I feel I can do to contribute to our agreed-upon goal?" This prompt is designed to help everyone see that just as they can all contribute to the problem, they can also all contribute to the solution. You're going right into this prompt without specifically addressing the issues raised in the first prompt yet.

This is intentional. This allows the group to see the problems for what they are and immediately take care of addressing the easy stuff. They will find that with some simple adjustments, and through the sheer power of the reminder of the basic nonnegotiable, they can go a long way toward helping to resolve the issues raised.

The next step, then, is to discuss those issues raised by the first prompt that were not resolved by the second prompt. It's unlikely, for example, that any teacher who is generally ineffective is going to respond to the second prompt by miraculously agreeing to revamp their teaching approach. In that case, it will be important for you to remind folks of the process that is used for teacher evaluation. Reassure everyone that it is your intention to continue (or begin if that's the honest state of affairs for you) to be vigilant about observing instruction and providing support to teachers with the intended goal of improving instruction and, therefore, the learning opportunities for students.

It's important that individual teachers do not take it upon themselves to be the judge and jury, so to speak, on one of their peers. Instead, trust that the leadership team will take the appropriate action here. This targeted discussion point is crucial for everyone and especially the Mrs. Folans of the group. You want her to understand that the general lack of effectiveness that was the reason for your initial conversation has not been overshadowed by the adult interaction concerns she raised at that time. You will be coming back to her to talk about teaching and learning.

You will also acknowledge here that the next whole-group discussion will be about the PLC model. It has become clear to you that it is not having the intended impact in this department, and you will make a commitment to working closely with the group to provide the professional development necessary to improve. This will involve assessing the current state of the PLCs both at the group level and at the individual teacher level, identifying areas for improvement, and then building professional development to address those areas. Your direct involvement in the department's PLCs, as well as that of your leadership team, will go a long way toward increasing effectiveness.

This is also a good time to address the generational issues that contribute to how individual teachers approach their classrooms. As this is probably not an issue that is isolated to your foreign language department, consider sharing that you will address this school-wide, though feel free to give some highlights here. A great exercise to address the generational issue is to put together a quick presentation that spotlights the characteristics of the different generations represented on your school team.

The simple act of seeing these characteristics brings an almost immediate sense of greater understanding; teachers realizing that the folks from other generations aren't just "being" a certain way but, instead, have actually been molded this way based on the simple fact of the time period they grew up in. When completing a similar exercise in other schools, we've used this example of the lack of understanding that comes with simply looking through the lens of your generation:

Mrs. Roberts has been teaching for twenty-five years. Her classroom is marked by order. The desks are in rows, every pencil has its place, students raise their hands to leave their seats. . . . You get the picture. Today she was walking up the hall and happened to pass Ms. Harp's room. She "heard" the class before she saw it because there was so much noise coming from the room.

In addition to the music that was playing, Mrs. Roberts could hear students talking and laughing. As she walked by, she saw students up and about the room. Desks were grouped together and students were standing and sitting on desks; even a few sat on the floor. Ms. Harp was bouncing from group to group and, from Mrs. Roberts's perspective, very little work was being accomplished.

As she continued up the hall, Mrs. Roberts made a mental note to avoid group work. Upon entering the teacher workroom, she announced to anyone siting there that "someone should get that new teacher, Ms. Harp, some help because her class was out of control."

This example achieves exactly what you want it to achieve. You start off with a little levity and specifically bring into focus the misinterpretations that can arise because of our specific lenses. Once you've shared this or a similar example and the characteristics of the generations, have everyone self-identify their generation.

Now have them get into mixed groups (i.e., you can't be in a group that has more than one other person from your same generation) and discuss how these characteristics play out in the classroom. As a final step, have the small groups share out their "aha" moments to the whole group and then sum up the importance of keeping your generational lenses, as well as those of the people on your team, in mind as you move forward.

Now that you've filled in the gaps between the first and second prompts, your final discussion point is to agree on next steps. Be sure that your next steps are specific. Be sure that they involve everyone. Be sure that there is a monitoring component built in (what gets monitored gets done). Be sure that you identify a follow-up meeting date and time so that it is clear that you intend to continue to be a part of the solution process.

On a final note, keep in mind that the structure outlined here, though specific with the vignette provided, can be generalized to fit many of the challenging situations that will arise in your school that require a courageous conversation (whether one on one, small group, large group, etc.). Also, you've likely noticed that I didn't build in a specific "say something that we do well" piece. It is not our intention to suggest you not discuss the positives, and you are encouraged to build that in as you see fit.

In this instance, given the nature of the concerns, you may see that the department discussion was already going to be lengthy. As an alternative, you might start out by offering a quick summary of positives before launching into your framework rather than having everyone offer their own. You may decide to build in a "one glow, one grow" piece. Again, this is your call. Keep in mind what you know about attention spans and then proceed from there.

Vignette II: School Resource Officer

Deputy Ludwig has been assigned as the school resource officer (SRO) here for six years. In his tenure, he has worked hard to build relationships with students and to gain the trust of staff and parents. Deputy Ludwig has been known to partner with the school leadership team in an effort to address the negative choices of students in a manner that is most likely to result in students learning from their mistakes and yet maintaining their dignity within the school environment.

Recently the deputy became aware that three students were questioned about and found to be in violation of the school's alcohol policy. The three students came to school under the influence of alcohol and came to the attention of the assistant principal, Ms. Conrad, during the first period of the day. Ms. Conrad investigated the incident and followed all school procedures. That said, one step is always to notify the SRO so that he can file the appropriate reports. It is understood that the SRO will not file charges against students unless the behavior is part of a pattern of negative choices.

In this instance, Ms. Conrad failed to report the incident after being distracted with another situation and in the absence of the SRO as he was out for training. Two days later, upon his return to the school, the SRO became aware of the incident and went to the principal, questioning why a report had not been made.

When counseled by the principal to speak with the assistant principal directly, Mr. Ludwig confronted the assistant principal and verbally reprimanded her for her failure to report. Ms. Conrad became defensive and tried to explain herself but was shut down by Mr. Ludwig's refusal to hear her explanation. After the verbal reprimand, Ms. Conrad went to her principal to discuss the situation and ask that the principal correct the SRO's behavior.

The school principal now has to weigh how to approach the situation. Technically, the SRO is not an employee of the school district. Instead, he is a representative of the sheriff's office, and their relationship hangs in the balance of a memo of understanding. Though she believes the SRO was out of line, she does not want to escalate the situation and risk the school's long-standing positive rapport with the SRO and the sheriff's office.

*(**Unintended consequence:** The principal's bookkeeper has an adjacent office and so is privy to many private conversations. She has heard both conversations and is concerned about her interpretation that the principal seems to treat the SRO with kid gloves. She believes he has overstepped his bounds in reprimanding the assistant principal and discusses this with another secretary at lunch. The two quickly agree that the principal's decision here will be an indicator of whether she will side with school staff in tough situations. The principal is relatively new to the school, and her decisions are under constant scrutiny.)*

Alternative Approach to Vignette II: School Resource Officer

The SRO is in a unique position wherein the local sheriff's department assigns a deputy to a school or cluster of schools to be a part of the safety structure for those schools. The SRO is employed by the sheriff's office and reports directly to a supervisor there. Technically, the SRO is not required to attend any staff meetings, trainings, and so on.

This makes it difficult to provide training on, say, power struggles, to the SRO and those in positions like his. This is where the relationships that the school leader builds with stakeholders become invaluable. These relationships are at the center of the culture of the school. A strong relationship can result in the SRO offering to attend such trainings in order to be better versed at supporting the school community.

Take Deputy Ludwig, for example. The principal in this scenario is new and is still fostering relationships. Her rapport with the SRO is positive thus far but has also not been particularly tested. In the future, the power struggle outlined here between the SRO and assistant principal can be avoided if the SRO attends the same training and the two adults approach the situation with a joint commitment to keeping everyone's dignity intact.

Keep in mind that the reality is that police officers have a completely different approach to the school environment than does school staff. Their training and purpose are unique to law enforcement. Melding the two worlds takes patience, partnership, and a willingness to look at situations that arise from different viewpoints.

Without shared training, the original confrontation between the SRO and assistant principal likely will not be avoided. This brings us then to the power struggle that ensues between adults when both the SRO and assistant principal vie for the principal's support, creating a situation where, potentially, one has to win while the other loses. The principal, when originally approached by the SRO, attempted to foster a conviction to solve the problem by advising the SRO to speak with the assistant principal directly rather than simply reporting the incident to the principal and awaiting her action.

Unfortunately, the principal missed the opportunity to offer guidance to the SRO about how to have the conversation, which would be prudent, especially given the SRO's emotional involvement at the time. His feelings of being overlooked or, worse, being intentionally left out of the information loop, are real for him, and the principal should have considered that, unchecked, these emotions would likely cause the conversation to take a negative turn.

In a redo, the principal might encourage the conversation while also reassuring the SRO that the oversight was not intentional (this can be proven by the principal sharing that the assistant principal did report to her as required) and reminding the SRO of the heretofore positive rapport held between him and Ms. Conrad. In doing so, she gives the SRO a chance to exercise strategy 4 (delaying the conversation), even if it is unknowingly done on his part. Essentially, the principal is now guiding the conversation while still empowering the SRO to have it himself. Again, this is a delicate balance, as the SRO does not likely feel he needs guidance. Subtlety is a must here.

The principal, if time allows, might also alert the assistant principal that the conversation is coming. Again, the goal is not for the principal to micromanage the situation. It is, however, an unmistakable teachable moment. The principal might simply let Ms. Conrad know that the SRO is upset and encourage her to have a listening ear and to simply reassure the SRO that she will continue to keep him in the loop in the future. By offering guidance to both parties, the principal is cultivating a culture of success.

If the principal's guidance succeeds in preventing the confrontation and, instead, a positive discussion ensues, then the unexpected consequence of the bookkeeper who questioned the principal's allegiance is avoided. Let's say, for argument's sake, however that it's not. This unexpected consequence is also not unusual. Having witnessed the conflict from her position, the bookkeeper now has some solid concerns about how the principal will side here. Of course, therein lies the problem, the fact that the bookkeeper believes that there are sides to be taken at all.

WRAP-UP

This brings us back, again, to the importance of all staff being included in training experiences about power struggles and all being very clear on your beliefs about this school culture. There cannot be "Us" and "Them." We are in this together, even when we don't see eye to eye and the responsibility lies within each of us to foster a sense of collaboration, a sense that we will support one another, and we will focus on the solution that promotes a positive school culture. When this "We" culture is created, the concern exhibited by the bookkeeper is avoided altogether.

Chapter Seven

Leading the Learning with Your Students

Coaching Your Students to Avoid Power Struggles

Our focus thus far has been on the adults in schools and strategies to use to ensure that they have a positive impact on your school's culture. It's only natural, then, that we would also spend time with the students. Your students' response to the tone set by the adults is another key component to your culture as a whole.

In earlier chapters, we made the argument that adults are at the core of your culture because of their role in shaping and developing all of the processes, procedures, and routines that make up your school day. We discussed that since your staff creates the processes, procedures, and routines, all of these are directly impacted by your staff's beliefs, therefore placing your staff's beliefs at the core of your culture. So where do the kids fit in?

Your students navigate each and every day in a cycle of response to the processes, procedures, and routines that have been established and, therefore, the beliefs that have been deemed the norm by your team. Right from the start, they will arrive at school and at class at a specified time, eat lunch at a specified time in a specified place, wear (or not wear) specific clothes, and even use the bathroom at specified times in some cases. Think about it. There's not much a student does during the course of the day that is not overseen by adults in some way. Thus, their contribution to your culture, for the most part, is via their response to all of these experiences.

In this chapter, we are going to focus on two ideas. The first idea centers on how to empower your students to be a part of the heretofore adult work of creating and implementing the processes, procedures, and routines that make up a school day. In doing so, your students' beliefs now also become a part of the equation that is the foundation for your school culture. Our second area of focus will be on how to prepare your students to mitigate and avoid power struggles just as you've done for the adults. Let's get started.

IT STARTS WITH YOU: THE LEARNING

Stop for a moment and answer these simple questions: How is the student voice heard in your school? What evidence can you provide of this? Your response to these questions will vary based on your school's context. Your response to these questions may vary due to the core beliefs held by you and your school team. We're not just talking about those beliefs that you wear on your sleeves; we're also talking about those beliefs that become evident through your work.

So what exactly are we getting at? Well, the fact is that most, if not all, schools have mission statements that directly state how they will provide a wonderful education for every child. This mission statement, when taken literally, often implies that students are at the forefront of our every decision, our every purpose. And most, if not all, schools mean it. But the great schools, the schools truly committed to the whole child and truly committed to producing global, lifelong learners (yes, language you often see in mission statements), are the schools where the student body actually has its own distinct voice.

If you're unsure of where you stand with student voice, ask yourself this question: If you asked your students to explain your school's mission and vision, the basic beliefs that you uphold, could they? Another strong barometer is whether you see students deliberately included in your "power" committees and teams—by that we mean those groups of people who truly have the authority to make decisions for the school. Still another barometer is, which students are celebrated and recognized in your school?

These are tough questions, no doubt, but your answers to them, your honest, non-sugar-coated answers to them are your truest gut check on this topic. You've been great about conducting your gut checks up to this point; don't stop now. Based on your responses to these prompts, you can either continue with the learning here in Part A or, if you've determined that your school is a model for student voice, then proceed ahead to the learning in Part B.

THE LEARNING: PART A

By now you can anticipate that our focus on ensuring that students are an integral part of how your school culture centers on the idea of student voice.

We'll define student voice as the way in which students are represented in your school; how their feelings, beliefs, and ideas are heard and included in your school setting. As with all things culture related, your effort to ensure that student voice is included has to be deliberate.

This doesn't happen by accident. Our experience actually suggests that in schools where there are no deliberate structures for student voice, you often see higher rates of disciplinary infractions, lower rates of student involvement in extracurricular activities, higher rates of absenteeism and, as a result, lower student achievement overall. Those are some pretty hefty prices to pay for overlooking or disregarding student voice.

So how do you correct the course mid-stream? First and foremost, we suggest acknowledging the problem. Start by asking your staff the same questions you answered above. Their answers will be similar to yours. Well, most of them will answer similarly. Be prepared for the group who will insist this isn't an issue and that no time needs to be spent on it. When that group rears their confrontational head, simply acknowledge their position and ask them to "play along" while you look at the data. Perhaps after that they will feel differently.

Now, present the entire team with the data—disciplinary data, attendance data, extracurricular enrollment data, and any other that you feel would be applicable. Perhaps your data screams that there is a problem. Maybe your data isn't terrible but suggests there is room for improvement. Regardless, make the link then between this data and your current student achievement.

Now make the suggestion to your team that addressing student voice, improving the ways in which students contribute to forming the school culture, will lead to improved achievement and a more positive school culture. Make sense? Ultimately, as school leaders we know that creating the opportunity for student voice is a moral obligation in schools. That said, focusing the conversation on improved achievement is most likely the tactic that will sway the naysayers.

Okay, you've made your case; now it's time to act. Your first step will be to query both your staff and students about ways in which they believe students could become more actively involved at the culture-building level of the school. This means finding specific ways that students can contribute to the creation and modification of processes, procedures, and routines. There are a myriad of ways to do this, but to jumpstart your team's brainstorming, we've shared some here.

Strategy 1: Students on Power Committees

Earlier, we defined power committees as those groups in your school that truly have the power to make decisions both at small levels and at the whole-school level. Examples of these committees in most schools include the school leadership team, school improvement team, honor code committee, and the staff advisory committee. You likely have others or different groups so take time now to identify what these groups look like in your school. We define these groups here.

- **School leadership team**—team in the school composed of the admin team plus other key stakeholder representatives like department heads, grade-level leads, parent representatives, student representatives, and so on. Ideally, this team handles all things instructional with no crossover into managerial topics that can distract from the focus on instruction.
- **School improvement team**—team in the school composed of representation similar to the school leadership team but with a specific focus on the school's improvement process. Oftentimes districts and states have specific processes that schools follow in order to identify growth goals, determine action to address those goals, and monitor the school's progress toward achieving those goals. Ideally this team oversees and monitors this process.
- **Honor code committee**—composed similarly to the two above, this team oversees a formal process identified by the school to address honor code violations. This can include anything from plagiarism, cheating on assignments, or otherwise breaking of rules that involve agreed-upon honor behavior.
- **Staff advisory committee**—composed similarly to the above groups, this team addresses anything school-wide that doesn't directly involve instruction. Some examples of areas of focus might include general school policies like dress code, attendance, tardiness, hallway traffic and monitoring, as well as any other topics the members bring to the table on behalf of their representative groups.

As you review these definitions and/or the groups you have in your school and their defined roles, doesn't it become glaringly obvious how important it is to have students involved? And just like with your staff representation, not just any student but students who you know will be able to represent their peers without being intimidated by the adults in the group. We cannot overstate this point enough—have a process in place whereby students can volunteer to be peer representatives and then can be vetted by your staff to ensure they will be effective in the role.

As the school leader, your responsibility, once students are selected, is to take the time with each one to make them familiar with the group/team and its purpose, introduce them to key staff in the group in order to begin to create a sense of familiarity, and assign them a staff mentor from the group who will make a point of sitting next to the student in the beginning, ensuring the student understands various topics, and in general will provide direct support during meetings until the student is comfortable on his or her own. To this point, also consider that assigning multiple students to groups/teams could be helpful in that they will likely be more comfortable with another student present.

Your final responsibility in this action to include student voice is to introduce the student to the whole team to which he is assigned and clearly articulate for everyone his role as you envision it. If left to figure this out on their own, your staff will come up with as many iterations as there are group members. Be clear up front and the student then has the maximum opportunity to actually have a voice in the group versus simply showing up as the token student representative.

Strategy 2: School Leader Active Role in Student Government

A second strategy to consider is the reverse of the first. In addition to getting students involved on power committees, it's important for you, the school leader, to become involved in student groups—especially your student government. What is your school's structure for student government? Is your student government one group that is composed of representatives from each grade? Is it multilayered in that each grade level has its own set of officers? Is it nonexistent?

How are your student officers chosen? Are they elected by other students or selected by adults? Does the selection process tend to be a popularity contest or a true reflection of each student's strengths and weaknesses? Your answers to these questions are key to your reflection on the role of student government in your school. Your goal, of course, is to have a lead student group truly selected for their talents and formally included in decisions that can impact school culture.

That leads us to our second line of questioning. How does your student government operate? What school-wide responsibilities do they hold? How do you hold them accountable for these responsibilities? Do they tend to only cover the more superficial things like running the school store at the elementary school or organizing homecoming events at the high school, or are you harnessing their knowledge and skills for topics that have a greater impact on your culture?

Again, your responses to these prompts will be a guide for you on how to meet your student government structure where it is and help move it in the direction of becoming a stronger, more substantive structure. You are not alone in this work and can certainly access a variety of resources online for ideas.

Suffice it to say, while you are overhauling your student government model or simply tweaking it, given our points of thought, you will also begin exploring your new role with the group. Just as there is power added to the student voice when they become involved in power committees, so too is power added when the school leader becomes actively engaged in the student government. No, this doesn't mean that you get to run for student president. Sorry, that dream is over.

It does mean, however, that you will develop a regular opportunity to engage with the group. Depending on their meeting schedule, you will request the opportunity to sit in for a part of it at a frequency that you all feel is appropriate and will be effective. This becomes a balance between being present enough to hear their collective voice but not so much as to stunt their voice.

Your purpose in these discussions is twofold. First, you will bring news to the group. Your news might include a heads-up about any student-specific issues on the horizon, perhaps a heads-up on changes in policies and practices—think planning for the next school year and how much respect you show for kids when you actually bring their student government into the loop on any changes and/or what to expect.

Your sharing might also involve soliciting the group to help in different areas. One quick example would be to get the students involved in the age-old debate about dress code. Instead of having the adults in the building continue to hammer this one home every year, why not get the student government to work on the message—they could create a great video to show their peers, decide on a marketing campaign to address the issue, and so on.

We know, we know . . . it's hard to let go of an issue upon which you love to spend so much of your time (insert sarcastic tone here). Seriously, though, the kids will do a far more creative job in getting the message out and, frankly, their peers will "hear" them better than they have ever heard you in the past.

The second purpose is to be a listener to the student government group on issues for which they need your support and guidance. This is a deliberate, regularly scheduled time when they know they will have your undivided attention (hint, hint . . . leave the radio off) to ask for your opinion on upcoming events or other things they are planning. It's also their opportunity to offer their insight to you about issues they see brewing in their peer group that may be falling under the radar of the adults. Imagine the strength you give to the student voice when you embark on becoming engaged with the student government body and the message you send to them and the adults in the building about the importance of honoring the beliefs of all.

Strategy 3: Assessing Your Approach to Student Recognition

All too often, schools tout the success of certain students/groups as their evidence that student recognition is alive and well in their schools. And yet when you scratch below the surface, what you really see is that really only a few students are actually the focus of the attention. Take a quick assessment.

Walk down your main foyer, or whatever your spot is in your building where you house all of the awards won by various students for various reasons. What do you see? Are the recognitions here reflective of your entire student body? Do you have the debate team awards front and center with the football team? Does your award-winning basketball team upstage your award-winning improvisation group? What about your National Merit Scholars? Do they even make the cut to have space here?

Fact is, in many schools, the athletic teams tend to upstage, well, everyone. It's an old-school approach that is still very much prevalent. In this model, student academic achievement accolades are completely absent. The good news is that all of our talk about school culture in the last twenty years has begun to result in some change here. This change is critical to student voice because an unbalanced approach to student recognition results in some student groups left feeling overlooked and invisible. Overlooked and invisible are detrimental to any sense of student voice.

Thankfully we are starting to see some model examples of schools that are thoughtful each and every time an accolade is earned by their students and that seek to determine the best integration of the accolade into the overall school picture. One great example is the idea of a changing mural in the awards area. Mounting document-sized Plexiglas rectangles in a particular area and giving the designated spot a changing theme can do this.

For example, perhaps for a bit you spotlight a picture of every student who earned a perfect score on your state test or, even better, was most improved in their scores from one year to the next. Another spotlight could be for National Merit Scholars over the years. Still another spotlight might be the kids who won the classroom- or school-level spelling or geography bees. You get the idea; it's a chance to recognize so many more academic areas and at all levels—not just the kids who go on to win it all.

What about your non–athletic competition teams? Though sometimes kids cross over between athletic and other competition teams, lots of times there is no crossover. That means that if your halls are only decked with athletic awards, then a whole, frequently large, portion of your student body has no hope of ever making the wall. If you're finding at this point that perhaps your school's physical acknowledgment space is more traditional than you first thought, then now is the time for an overhaul.

Tie this process in with the first strategies here and use your targeted teams and committees to assess and make some decisions in this area. Your target goal is to create a space where every student who walks through can see someone who "looks like me," someone who has similar areas of interest and/or talents and, as a result, makes me feel like I, too, am doing something that our school values.

Let's shift our focus now from the physical to the less physical. Changing gears, let's spend some time thinking about your system of awards and recognitions. We know how important it is to take time out throughout our school year to celebrate success. We discussed this earlier in chapter 6 as it relates to the adults in the school. But what about the students? Consider the student recognition systems you already have in place.

Perhaps you have quarterly or annual awards presentations. What is your focus? Do you seek to recognize the achievements of the whole child or solely focus on one area? Our recommendation, of course, is that schools expand any singular approach to include the whole child. Though academic achievement should always be our primary focus, its important to also herald the importance of character, leadership, and a sense of community responsibility.

Once you better understand in what areas you will target your recognition, move to who gets recognized. Do you find that your awards ceremonies tend to result in a small handful of students being selected over and over again? If so, it's time to take a note from schools that have evolved in this area. We aren't arguing the fact that in every grade level there tend to be your standouts. These are the kids who have the highest achievement year after year, tend to be favored by teachers year after year, and, as a result, tend to get the entire spotlight year after year.

If you're not sure if you meet this criterion, ask your students. Seriously, they'll tell you. Let's face it, after about the third or fourth grade, they tend to have a sense of their "place" in their grade-level group. Likewise, they can almost begin to predict each year who the kids are that will earn the awards. This becomes frustrating and devaluing especially if you're the kid who is next in line. You're also bright, you're also hardworking. . . . That Susie just happens to have a slight edge on you. Yet year after year, that slight edge results in her being the superstar and you going unnoticed and unrecognized.

Just like we discussed with the physical awards and recognitions, so too is the award ceremony process a hotbed for student voice. If you sit by year after year and watch the same kids get the awards, doesn't it stand to reason that you begin to feel invisible? No matter how hard you worked this year, you know that the award is always going to Susie. Heck, maybe next year you won't work so hard if you have learned that your hard work will go unnoticed no matter what.

What to do, what to do? It's quite simple actually. You've heard this common theme throughout this resource—be deliberate. Be deliberate. Yes, it takes more time. Yes, it means breaking a vicious cycle. Yes, we can promise you it will be worth it.

So what does it look like? Here's what happens. As you plan for your awards cycle in the coming school year, go ahead and approach this very important work like you do all other big decisions, and have it become a product of a standing team—preferably your school leadership team. This team's primary focus is academics, just as the primary focus of your awards is academic. Set a new intention by sharing the learning in this chapter and suggesting that this year the intent will be to recognize a larger group of learners, not just the obvious superstars.

To that end, each department or grade level is tasked with two objectives when choosing their awards recipients: first, choose the top three students for any given award and rank them from one to three (let's say the outstanding math student award as an example). Next, compare that list with the previous year's award recipient list—were any of these the same students recognized in their previous grade? If so, reprioritize the list so that a nonrecipient from the previous year becomes the top choice for this year.

After each grade level, department, and so forth has come up with their lists, the team reconvenes to finalize. One by one, each award is identified along with the top selectee. Once a student has been chosen for one award, all other groups have to take him or her off their list (assuming there are duplications) and choose another student from their top three for the award. So, for example, your math department's selectee for the outstanding math student award can no longer be in contention for the other awards.

There are those who will believe that if a student works hard and earns it, then he should get as many awards as folks want to give him. We get it. There are those students who are just that good. That said, when you really look closely, what you find is just behind that student, maybe even by a mere decimal point, is another student who is just as outstanding.

Doesn't she deserve recognition as well? Yes, now we're getting into your team's beliefs about awards and punishment. Yes, you may have to stop long enough to hash out those beliefs. Isn't that a powerful conversation to have with your staff? Won't it be even more powerful now that you are factoring in student voice in these committees, and they can share their beliefs as well?

In the end, this piece is about suggesting that the act of awarding over and over again the same group of students can ultimately stunt growth. We all know that "those" kids—the superstars, will be superstars no matter what. That said, the students right behind them, well, their potential for rising to super-star level increases exponentially when they are given the opportunity to share the spotlight. Just like their likelihood to allow their success to slowly dissipate, their even subconscious inclination to work a little less hard has the potential to negatively impact their performance and success over time.

Okay, that's three strategies to use to begin the work of increasing the student voice in your school. Though they are just a beginning, you can see that they each have the potential to drastically increase the role of your students' beliefs across your entire school picture. This, folks, is where the rubber meets the road regarding school culture.

THE LEARNING: PART B

Let's turn our attention now to how to approach our students regarding power struggles. If it takes two people for a power struggle to ensue, as we discussed in earlier chapters, then it makes sense that we would provide the opportunity for students to better understand power struggles and ways to ensure they don't end up in a situation they simply cannot win. Just as with adults, students involved in power struggles lose.

Sure, there may be times when a student feels like he's won because he "saved face" in front of his friends. Even then, though, that sense of winning only lasts a moment. Ultimately, he realizes that to save face he had to hurt someone else. By engaging in the power struggle, he'll pay the price of a disciplinary consequence; even worse, by pushing back, he ended up painting himself as a student with a disrespectful attitude, an image that will take a while to mend with some of his more favored teachers. As we said earlier, in a power struggle, everyone loses.

Just as with the adults, we take time with the students at the start of the year to set the tone about expectations. We give them advice about how to handle conflicts with staff—especially conflicts where they think they have been treated unfairly or disrespectfully. It is with these conflicts that power struggles most often arise.

Just as with adults, this is best done in small groups (advisory group is a great setting). That said, it's important that the message not be swayed by others and/or not be diluted by the sheer fact that so many different folks conveyed it. To that end, consider a video lesson incorporating both your leadership team and student leaders (that, perhaps, can be viewed in advisory with the advisory teachers leading a follow-up Q&A scripted by your leadership/student leadership team).

Remember, as always, that this is a great time for you to lead by example and create a true lesson that incorporates all of the facets you expect of your teachers. Your student leadership members will be able to help you tailor the lesson in a way to ensure that it's engaging.

Likewise, have them take an active role in leading the learning for their peers. In the context of the lesson, you will provide specific strategies for students to use when dealing with a power struggle. We suggest using the same strategies outlined for teachers in the lesson in chapter 8. These strategies apply across all ages and can be used by your students whether they're dealing with power struggles with school staff, their parents, or even their peers.

In addition, however, you'll want to send a specific message to students with respect to your expectations about interactions with school staff. Here are three strategies to teach students:

1. Most struggles arise over a breach of school rules—so follow the rules and you're good. And remember, we do recognize that some of the rules may not make sense to you or are inconsistently applied. If you don't like a rule, we have a process for having it reviewed for potential change. Side note: if you don't have such a process in your school, get one. Again, this leads to students having a sense of voice in their school.

   Adults who act as though everything they create is 100 percent accurate all of the time are not setting a good example for kids. Instead, with a process to formally and respectfully question a rule or policy, you send the message to your kids that no one is perfect and that rules and policies are always in a constant state of evolution. You also send the message that collaboration results in greater gains for everyone.

2. Know yourself and your ability to deal with conflict. If you know that the person talking to you is someone with whom you don't see eye to eye, agree to their request and then talk to a trusted adult about the problem (Note how this ties in to our earlier discussion about understanding how connected your students are to the adults in the building. This strategy doesn't work if the connection piece is not in place). That adult will work with you (and an administrator/counselor if necessary) to find a solution.

   Students figure out fairly quickly who among the adult staff can push their buttons easily. Some students will engage these adults on purpose to trigger the power struggle and subsequent attention it entails. On the other hand, some of these adults are also guilty of deliberately pushing the buttons. Including this strategy sends the message to all that you are committed to eliminating power struggles, no matter the reason.

3. Understand your body language and the body language of others. If you feel yourself exhibiting signs that can be construed as disrespectful, then that is a good time to back off, end the conversation politely, and go seek assistance from another adult. Your message to students is simple; if you engage in a power struggle with an adult, you will lose; translated, you will likely end up with a consequence for insubordination (technically both people lose, but it's important for kids to see it as a no-win situation, in hopes that we can avoid the power struggle all together).

The better option is to resist the power struggle and seek out support to resolve the issue. Ultimately give your kids this out—when an adult in our school asks you to do something (short of doing something you feel is ethically or morally wrong or could cause harm), do it. If you feel the adult treated you disrespectfully or that the situation was unjust or unfair, talk to someone you trust later, and work through it together.

In keeping with our previous chapters, let's take a look at a couple of power struggle scenario that you may find helpful when creating your lesson for kids. Keep in mind that role-playing, though likely to cause kids of most ages to roll their eyes, is still a powerful learning strategy—especially when practicing how to have tough conversations with adults.

Vignette I: Remember Lindsey from Chapter 3?

Lindsey is a sixth grader at a suburban middle school. As a first-time middle schooler, she has struggled with staying organized. She's still adjusting to multiple teachers and multiple classes and finds that there are times when she forgets homework assignments. Add to that, she is overextended.

She is on two sports teams, and she dances. The pull of so many after-school practices is starting to take its toll. Missing homework has never been a problem in the past, and she's embarrassed to ask for help. Couple that with the fact that Lindsey is quick to become defensive with adults, and we find that Lindsey tends to comes across as intentionally disrespectful.

Lindsey is dreading going to first period today. She didn't complete her entire homework assignment in science, and she knows Ms. Tally is a stickler for "full completion = credit." She has tried in the past to get Ms. Tally to compromise with no luck. More and more, first period feels like a battle-ground with Lindsey and Ms. Tally pitted against one another.

At the start of class, Ms. Tally directs students to take out their homework and put it on their desk for her to check. As she moves from student to student, she simply picks up each sheet to see that both sides have been completed. When Ms. Tally arrives at Lindsey's desk, she finds a half-completed assignment. "Lindsey, you didn't finish your homework, so you can't get credit." Lindsey, seemingly just waiting for the power struggle to begin, responds, "That's not fair. I did part of it so I should get part credit." "You know my policy," Ms. Tally responds. "All or none." "That doesn't make any sense," Lindsey replies, "all you're doing is checking it off. You're not even checking to see if anyone got the answers right." Ms. Tally responds firmly "Lindsey, I'm not going to argue with you" and moves on to the next student.

Lindsey's agitation increases as she looks around and sees, once again, that all eyes are on her. Some students are laughing and whispering while others are just shrugging as if to say, "Nothing you can do about it." Lindsey calls out to Ms. Tally again. "Ms. Tally I still don't think it's fair that I'm not getting any credit. If you'd look at my sheet, you'd see that at least my answers are correct and at least I did my own work. I know you know some kids copy each other's work in the locker area in the mornings, and you just give them credit anyway without doing anything to stop it. I don't get it. What's the point if we're not going to check it and make sure we got things right."

Ms. Tally takes the bait and launches into her usual explanation about the importance of practice and of learning time management and taking responsibility as a learner. Lindsey continues to counter with assertions about how practice doesn't work if there is no review and you don't know what you did right or wrong.

This back-and-forth sparring continues as Ms. Tally circulates in the room and continues to check homework. Eventually, other students begin to grumble and comment under their breath in agreement with Lindsey. Ms. Tally finally brings an end to it by announcing, "Fine, if you all don't like my homework policy, then tell me why. For homework tonight each of you is to write a five hundred-word essay on why homework is important. I want you to really think about it and come up with at least one reason. No exceptions."

Alternative Approach to Vignette I: Remember Lindsey from Chapter 3?

Given this scenario and the strategies that you have now outlined with the students, how would you proceed? Consider having two members of your student leadership team role-play the scenario. One can be the teacher, and the other can be Lindsey. Provide each with the script above as well as a copy of the strategies you've recommended for kids. Ask them to act out the scenario.

When done, conduct a brief Q&A of the scenario. Include comments and questions like: Briefly discuss how you felt during the power struggle. What do you think the other person was trying to achieve/gain, from your perspective? What was actually achieved? Now focus on Lindsey's role and ask the two participants to review the strategies and choose an alternative approach. The key here is to remind students that they cannot control the adult or the adult's response; that's why we are focusing on an alternative to their own response. Focus on what you can control.

When they're ready, have them role-play again modeling the use of one of the strategies. Be prepared to coach them at first. You may need to suggest which strategy to use and/or show how more than one strategy could work. Consider also using a student-to-student example within the context of this learning process. Your student leadership group will have no problem at all providing you many examples of the types of power struggles they have with their peers. Likewise, they will give you feedback on how the three strategies listed above will fare as well as any additional strategies they'd like to recommend to peers to use in these types of situations.

WRAP-UP

Student voice is a critical factor in your school culture. Schools where student voice is minimized are easy to pick out. From the moment you walk in the front door, you can feel the lack of student input. Likewise, the data we discussed earlier almost always tells a similar story. Your efforts to change this in your school are a key step in your leadership development and, again, the opportunity model for your entire school community your commitment to a whole-school, whole-staff, and now whole-student approach to a positive school culture.

Chapter Eight

Leading the Learning

Your Professional Development Guide

Chapter 8 is about leading the learning; how you specifically support adults as they learn to eliminate the use of power struggles. This chapter is an actual lesson plan designed for your entire school team because every adult who has contact with students, either positively or negatively, shapes the learning environment and school experience. If at all possible, include bus drivers, custodians, cafeteria staff, and your school's resource officer.

As the leader and person in authority, coaching the staff is essential. It's more effective to address the topic in small groups (departments, PLCs, etc.) but certainly if your only opportunity is to address the whole-school team, please do so. Note that we use the following terms in our lesson plan template: Opener, Pre-assessment, Learning, Practice, and Formative assessment. You would change the language to match the language used by your team in their instructional plans. This is your opportunity to model those same expectations you've set for your team. Now let's get started with the lesson.

OPENER (SETTING THE STAGE)

In the Opener, specifically discuss the reasons (your motivation and goals) you want the team to discuss power struggles. Reflect back to chapter 2 for support here. Begin by sharing a personal experience, and then ask your team members to talk about their experiences with power struggles in pairs or triads to get them warmed up around the topic. Participants will probably agree that power struggles result in someone feeling a loss or lack of control or respect. Equally important is effectively communicating how these feelings of loss or lack of control have negatively impacted the student-learning environment in your school.

This is a great place to go to the data. Think back to chapter 1 where we talked about the "what" of school culture and how your stakeholders perceive the culture. Turn, then, to the "whys" and how your root cause analysis of the data has indicated power struggles as a key "why" behind some of the negative perceptions.

Again, this is an opportunity for you to model for staff. Specifically, you'll model the importance of making decisions based on data as well as how to drill down in the data to get to the "whys" that will then be a guiding force in mapping out the path on how to proceed.

PRE-ASSESSMENT: SCENARIO

Ask for a volunteer to share a past power struggle that didn't end up well. In other words, the adult felt that both parties walked away feeling disrespected and viewing the other person negatively. Be prepared, as always, to provide an example of your own as a starting point for those folks who feel they cannot come up with one. This would be a great place to use one of the vignettes you've read here. Give the team time to discuss the scenario in small groups, focusing on any portions they feel could be modified for a better outcome. Ask the team to keep the scenario in mind for discussion after the learning.

THE LEARNING

As always, be sure to start with the why. Why is it important to minimize power struggles in our school? Make it clear to your team that these negative feelings become the basis for a negative school culture. There is plenty of research that correlates a negative school culture to poor student achievement, lower teacher retention, and a general lack of community. If an adult is likely to engage in a power struggle with a student, they are also more likely to be confrontational with colleagues.

This, of course, directly impacts teaching and learning. Finally, a negative school culture is more likely to result in a generally unsafe school. Students who do not feel positive about their school are much more likely to break rules and make poor choices that can result in unsafe situations.

It's important for your team to understand and agree that a positive school culture is critical to student success and safety. Share the following recommendations on how to avoid power struggles. Ultimately, that is our goal. No one wins in a power struggle, and the goal is to eliminate these struggles and, thereby, avoid the negative feelings associated with power struggles.

To that end, we have to work toward increasing our capacity to not allow conflict to result in a power struggle. One key to all of these recommendations is that the adult always adopts a calm demeanor and soft tone when a potential power struggle arises. Just these two adjustments to his or her approach will go a long way toward preventing the power struggle from beginning. Keeping those two keys in mind, here are some recommendations on how to respond when faced with a situation that is likely to result in a power struggle.

1. *Offer choices:* Yes, it seems simple that adults and kids alike respond more positively to choices than demands. If you are in a situation where you want/need the student, parent, or colleague to do something specific, identify a way for the person to have a choice. It should go without saying that the choices shouldn't be "do what I say or go to the office." That tactic will not fool anyone and will only serve to escalate the situation. Instead, offer two choices that are centered on moving the situation to a mutually agreeable resolution.

2. *Avoid negative words:* No one wants to hear "No!" "You can't." "Stop!" "Do _____ or else . . . ," etc. These words can't always be avoided (especially when safety risks exist) but we can be thoughtful about not making them our "go-to" words. To that end, it's important to have the team identify some easy-to-remember positive go-tos instead. Practicing these positive go-tos may seem silly to some, but the fact is, practice will be needed especially for folks who are habitually guilty of going right to the negative words.

3. *Show understanding:* Adults don't always agree with the rules or processes, either, and yet we follow them anyway because we understand the root cause or reason. Share your personal sentiment and then why you follow the rule or process anyway. Be as specific as possible. Sharing your personal perspective demonstrates both respect and trust for the other person.

   You might also explain why the rule or process exists. Only do so, however, if you are 100 percent sure of your explanation. Making something up as you go can cause more damage than good in this situation. If you don't know the background of a rule or process, acknowledge that, and demonstrate a willingness to find out the information and circle back to the other person to discuss it.

4. *Delay your interaction:* If a student, parent, or colleague does something that immediately makes you angry, frustrated, or annoyed (again, short of a safety issue or anyone being at risk), don't immediately engage. We all know that going into a conversation with those

emotions only makes the situation worse. Even if the other person does what you ask, they are obeying but not respecting you as an authority and they won't internalize the request (they'll just do what they want instead in the future when you are out of sight).

In the case of the student or colleague, consider that this dynamic also makes it much more likely that you will have contributed to having a negative effect on the other person's ability to learn or teach in his or her next class. Think of it this way: no teacher appreciates it when a student walks into their classroom angry and hostile because of an interaction they just had with another adult (even when the adult is justified).

As an example, let's go back to our initial scenario in chapter 2. In that case, instead of approaching Derek in the moment, Mr. Smith could indicate he sees the hat (perhaps by pointing to his head) and say "Derek, I'll touch base with you later about the school dress code." In doing so, Mr. Smith acknowledges for Derek and others that he sees the infraction and intends to address it later in a private manner.

School leader note: This is a good time to determine two or three key things your team will agree to as the go-to statements for handling conflict with students. An important learning experience is to have staff members share statements/actions that they find work productively with students as well as those that don't. Once the brainstorming is complete, be concrete about which of these statements will be used by all team members.

5. *Be prepared to walk away:* In particularly challenging situations, be prepared to walk away. If you have tried other options (like those offered in numbers 1–4), and the other person is adamant about engaging in the power struggle, state, "I feel like we are headed toward a power struggle and, frankly, I'm not interested in going down that road. We both lose in that scenario and I don't want this to be negative."

   In the case of students, "I'll let your counselor/administrator know we talked and perhaps the three of us can touch base together to work this out for the future." In this instance, you are preserving the possibility of a relationship with the student while also letting him or her know that you are holding him or her to the expectation (which also sends a positive message—you know they're intelligent enough to get it done). Walking away in this manner is not a loss of power. It models for the student that sometimes the best resolution is one that is delayed until emotions calm down.

6. *Be proactive with recurring issues:* Long-term picture, address those issues as a school team that are repeated problems. The ugly truth is that the majority of schools constantly deal with the small stuff (hats,

short skirts, tardiness, etc.) and detest the time that is devoted to these trivial topics.

That's not to say that being on time to class is not critical. It is to say that in the mind of the student these small issues are absolutely trivial, and we are unlikely to make them see it otherwise. The most effective course of action is to harness the power of your school community—students, teacher, parents, and so on—to address the issue(s) head on versus fighting the battle every day with the same small group of students.

THE PRACTICE

Once you have thoroughly explored these ways to avoid power struggles, put the group into pairs and have them go back to their original scenario (either their own or the one provided by you) and reenact it using one or more of these methods. They can either talk through how to modify the scenario or do a role play of the scenario or you could have them write about it first and then share it with their partner. As a final practice, ask for a couple of volunteers to share their before/after scenarios, and allow the larger group to provide feedback. You may want to have members of your school leadership team prepared to go first.

Formative Assessment

Offer each team member an index card and ask him or her to indicate which of the methods discussed today will be one that he or she will try to use in a future instance of conflict with a student. On the back, ask each member to write one more suggestion to add to our list of methods to avoid power struggles. Compile this additional list and send out to your team after this session. This becomes your launching point for all future conversations and follow-up learning and practice for staff.

FINAL THOUGHTS

Regardless of the outcome, a culture where power struggles are permitted to persist is a culture where students begin to learn the lesson that they always lose. Gone unaddressed, power struggles send the message that students can and will be targeted. The result—students begin to feel they have nothing to lose and are more likely to engage adults disrespectfully, discipline referrals increase, school safety decreases, and a cycle of a negative school culture is bred or continued. As the school leader, you have the moral responsibility to tackle the issue; and, with this book, you have some tools with which to begin the work.

Throughout this resource we have identified multiple starting points for your school team. Your intention is to build a collective mindset among your team so that the approach to power struggles is consistent. Your staff will look to you to see what the learning actually looks like in action. We encourage you to think each day about which small opportunities will present themselves, upon which you can build and model the learning. This ensures that you reinforce agreed-upon actions by practicing every day for all to see.

And finally, please remember this—your every action sends a message. And your lack of actions sends a message. When you knowingly allow power struggles to exist in your school, your school team and your students notice. They translate your lack of action as consent. Avoiding this sense of consent only occurs when you take deliberate, purposeful action.

About the Author

Janice Case is an educator with twenty-plus years of K–12 experience in both private and public school education. Most recently, Janice served as principal of Potomac Falls High School in Loudoun, Virginia. Her extensive public school experience includes serving as middle and high school principal, high school assistant principal, and special education teacher.

As a school leader, Janice was active at the state and national levels in her roles as state coordinator and executive board member for the Virginia Association of Secondary School Principals. She contributed to numerous committees and task forces, including task forces at both the state and national levels responsible for cultivating and implementing new teacher and principal evaluation standards and practices.

Janice has provided consultant services in professional development to schools and school leaders nationwide. She has collaborated with the National Association of Secondary School Principals, the National Institute for School Leadership, the Virginia Association of Secondary School Principals, the Virginia Foundation for Education Leadership, and the Virginia Department of Education to provide professional learning experiences on a wide range of topics targeted at supporting school leaders and teachers through the school transformation process. In addition, Janice works with her local school district as a leadership coach.

Janice lives in Oak Harbor, Washington, with her husband and two of their six children. In addition to her professional work, she is active in her local community through a variety of community-service endeavors, including being active on two local community boards committed to supporting military families.

Contact Information:
Janice Case
721 S.W. Castilian Drive
Oak Harbor, WA 98277
E-mail: j.caseconsultants@gmail.com
Phone: 904-705-7438